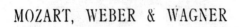

MOZART, WEBER & WAGNER

Berlioz

MOZART, WEBER AND WAGNER

WITH

VARIOUS ESSAYS ON MUSICAL SUBJECTS

BY

HECTOR BERLIOZ

TRANSLATED FROM THE FRENCH BY

EDWIN EVANS

WILLIAM REEVES
LONDON

Published by
WILLIAM REEVES Bookseller Ltd.,
1a Norbury Crescent, London, S.W.16

Made in England

First published in 1918
Reprinted 1969

PRINTED IN GREAT BRITAIN BY
LOWE AND BRYDONE (PRINTERS) LIMITED, LONDON

PUBLISHER'S NOTE

These essays and criticisms are taken from the volume published in French under the title "A Travers Chants, Etudes Musicales, Adorations, Boutades et Critiques". The remainder of "A Travers Chants" has been translated and published in two companion volumes entitled "Gluck and his Operas" and "Critical Study of Beethoven's Symphonies".

INDEX

(B) TO CONTENTS IN ORDER

INTRODUCTION

THE contents of the present portion of "A TRAVERS CHANTS" are not only extremely diverse, but, in the author's arrangement of them, are entirely unclassified. They might, however, have been easily so ordered as to show a natural division into three classes of criticism; and, but for a certain disrespect which this plan might have appeared to involve, it would have been adopted. Upon the whole, however, a middle course seemed to be the most advisable; that, namely, of preserving the original order of succession; but of utilising this opportunity in order to point out how an intellectual grasp of the whole may best be compassed.

I.—The first class of essay consists of the express criticisms written by Berlioz of the works of other composers, the foremost appearance in the present case being that of Weber; whose "Der Freyschütz" and, particularly, whose "Oberon," are here very fully discussed. Both dissertations are couched in a vein of criticism which is somewhat peculiar to Berlioz; and one which happily unites a light and entertaining—

often a humorous—manner with the very deepest thought and the most searching examination.

The attention herein given to Wagner appears to come next in the order of importance; the account of the Paris concerts, which took place at a time when that great composer was striving for a fuller recognition by the French public, having now an important added interest, as showing how greatly the conception of Wagner as founder of a "school of the future" had taken possession of the French mind; and, at the same time, as helping to explain the letter addressed by Wagner to Berlioz in protest against all such notions.* Whatever may then have been Berlioz's misconceptions, the present-day reader is not likely to take any other view than that they were sincere, if only for the reason that they were shared by the great majority of the musical public of most European countries; and it would have been strange, indeed, if Berlioz, a Frenchman, and, as Wagner apparently took a rather malicious interest in pointing out, ignorant of the German language, had been more accurately informed than many of Wagner's own countrymen.

---

* Berlioz had written his article in the capacity of critic to the "Journal des Debats," in which paper its original publication took place, on February 9, 1860; the letter of Wagner, in reply following, in the "Presse Théâtrale," on February 26 of the same year. Wagner's letter, being in French, appeared in translation in the "Neue Zeitschrift" for information of the German public; but, independently of that, Wagner gave his own translation in Vol. VII of the "Gesammelte Schriften."

The greatness of Mozart elevates the short paper devoted to an examination of his "Il Seraglio" to more importance than it would otherwise possess; but the reader is likely to find much interest in the happy conception of uniting the consideration of this work with that of Weber's "Abu-Hassan"; both operas being the productions of very youthful composers, and both being based upon Turkish subjects.

The paper upon the subject of Bellini's "Romeo" brings very strongly to light the depth of Berlioz's Shakespearean convictions; and, perhaps, also something of his weakness, in affecting a greater knowledge of English language and literature than he actually possessed. Already, in the treatment of Gluck's "Alceste," he had made the perversions of the tragedy of Euripides the object of his satire; but the bitterness of his expression in that instance falls considerably short of that devoted to the various corrupters of the work of Shakespeare; his indignation in the latter case leading him to cry out with Othello—"Are there no stones in heaven?"[*]

It is in the course of the essay on "Romeo" that occasion is found for incidental references to Steibelt, Delayrac and Zingarelli; and these, with the interesting paper on Reber's symphonies and Heller's pianoforte works, complete the portion of the present collection of articles more or less expressly devoted to a consideration of other composers.

---

[*] Act V, scene 2.

II.—The second class of essay is that addressed to abstract musical questions, and comprises five numbers; of which the papers upon "Church Music" (in shape of a review upon the work of d'Ortigue) and "The Pitch" (written for general enlightenment at the time when a commission had been appointed for consideration of this subject) are the most important. They are, in fact, worthy contributions to the literature of those matters; whilst the remaining effusions classed under this head—those, namely, relating to "modern instruments and ancient scores"; "high and low sounds"; and "Delsarte's tuning method" respectively, are merely fugitive, and of passing interest.

III.—The third class comprises various samples of a kind of criticism to which Berlioz was very greatly addicted, and in which he sought to expose the musical shortcomings of his countrymen and the general abuses to which his art was subject. It was in this style of writing that he both rose to his greatest height of literary excellence, and also fell to a distinct grade of inferiority. No one, for example, can read the "Address to Members of the Academy of Fine Arts" (which is the most important essay of the kind herein contained) without being struck both by its eloquence and by an occasional lapse into descriptions which mar the general effect. The genial mode of expression becomes thus an antidote—possibly even one upon which Berlioz himself may have relied—in order to induce the reader to pass lightly over literary traits to which he had not given much attention. The mem-

bers of the Institute, however, do not appear to have
been very charitably inclined as the paper was never
read at their public sittings; but that will not affect
the immense pleasure to be obtained from its perusal
by others less critical, and especially by those to whom
such a candid expression of a great musician's inner-
most thoughts cannot fail to be acceptable.

The satirical paper on "Chinese Musical Manners"
(which is the next of this category in order of importance) is an instance of Berlioz's witty manner; so
much so as to be more suitable for purposes of pure
amusement than valuable for any direct instruction
likely to be conveyed. The remaining chapters of
this class are of more or less subordinate interest; relating one and all to musical grievances. But these
are also one and all described with such general at-
tractiveness, and with so much interspersion of useful
information, that the reader may, if he will, desert
their main track, in favour of amusing detail. The
most important of the group is "Sunt Lacrymæ
rerum"; the others being respectively "The Time is
Near," "About a Faust-Ballet," "The Little-dog
School" and "To Be or Not to Be." The last, as a
paraphrase upon the soliloquy of Hamlet, is likely
to be the least welcome to English readers; though the
application of the form of Hamlet's monologue to the
musical grievances which Berlioz had in view to describe must be admitted as ingenious. This piece is
rather a notable instance of the desire to appear in
the eyes of Frenchmen as one well versed in Shakespear-

ean matters; a desire which is apparently also the cause of allusions to, and illustrations drawn from, Shakespeare being somewhat more frequent than required.

But, in spite of all, who can be found to say that this is not a most charming volume?—a kind of book of which there are marvellously few samples, for it is no less than its author's full confession. The single-mindedness which leads to ardency as well as the ardency which, in its turn, leads to an undue exuberance may perhaps be open to criticism from the more rigid standpoint; but to the sincere reader such theoretical flaws will appear to be of quite slight importance in comparison with the delight of being brought into such close communion with a master mind.

In conclusion, the translator feels called upon, once again, to give an account of his stewardship; although the observations made in introducing the other sections of this work here again apply. The lighter style of the present collection has, perhaps, slightly increased the difficulty of rendering the translation of equal warmth with the original, and correspondingly increased the temptation to an occasional circumlocution; all that can be said upon this point being that exercise of this privilege has been strictly limited to what appeared to be in the reader's interest. Shakespearean quotations have, of course, been referred to their original; whilst poetical extracts, though necessarily given in the original French, are all translated in foot-notes; and, where necessary to the elucidation, rhymed and rhythmised for that purpose.

MOZART, WEBER & WAGNER

I

THE ADDITION OF MODERN INSTRUMENTS
TO ANCIENT SCORES

IT was recently remarked, at one of the Conservatoire concerts, that, in the duet of Gluck's "Armide":

Esprits de haine et de rage

the voices were frequently overpowered by loud trom-
bone-notes, and thus lost much of their effect. These
trombone-parts, which are very indifferently done, have
been added at Paris, I do not know by whom; whilst,
at Berlin, this work has suffered to an even greater
degree from the same cause. Now, it may be useful
to observe, in connection with this subject, that, for
neither "Armide" nor "Iphigenia in Aulide," has
Gluck written a single note for trombones. It is useless to reply that, the reason for his abstaining from

B

the use of this instrument in "Armide" was because there were no trombones at the Opera at that time; for, in "Alceste" and "Orphée," both of which were represented before "Armide," those instruments appear, and, in the first of these, play a highly important part. Moreover, they are also employed in "Iphigenia in Tauride."

It is strange that a composer, however great he may be, should not be allowed to write for his orchestra as he chooses; and, especially, that he should not be free to abstain from the use of certain instruments whenever he sees fit to do so. It has admittedly happened in several instances, and even to illustrious masters, to correct the instrumentation of their predecessors; to whom they thus made a free gift of their learning and taste. Thus, Mozart added new accompaniments to the oratorios of Handel; but divine justice decreed that, later on, the operas of Mozart himself should be re-instrumented in their turn. This happened in England: where trombones, ophicleides and bass drums were thrust into the scores of "Figaro" and "Don Giovanni."

Spontini confessed to me one day that he had added, though admittedly with considerable discretion, wind parts to those which were already present in the score of "Iphigenia in Tauride," by Gluck. Two years afterwards, he was complaining bitterly, in my presence, of some excesses of this kind which he had witnessed; and of the abominable crudities added to the scores of dead masters, who were no longer there to defend themselves. Spontini exclaimed:

It is a shame! it is frightful! And I fear that they will correct me too, after I am dead.

—to which I could only sadly reply:

Alas! my dear master; have you not, yourself, already corrected Gluck?

Even the greatest symphonist the world has ever seen has not been allowed to escape from this indescribable kind of outrage; and, independently of the overture to "Fidelio," which they have "tromboned" from one end to the other in England (being of opinion forsooth that, in that overture, Beethoven's employment of trombones was too reserved) they have already commenced, in another quarter, to correct the instrumentation of the

C MINOR SYMPHONY!

I intend some day, in the form of a special article, to present you with the names of all these ravagers of works of art.

II

HIGH AND LOW SOUNDS; OR, THE EX-
TREMES OF THE KEYBOARD

ONE day, in listening to an opera, my attention was attracted by a *descending* scale, vocalised as a roulade, and set to the words:

Je roulais dans l'abime,*

the imitative intention of which I found to be of the most distinctly humorous kind.

It is obvious that, in the composer's idea, a descending roulade had become the musical equivalent of the movement of a tangible body rolling from high to low. The notes, as written upon the stave, certainly do represent a descending direction *to the eye*; but even this visible semblance would no longer exist if the system of figured music were to gain ascendancy. Moreover, should the executant, in reading, caprici-

---

* I rolled into the abyss.

4

ously choose to turn his music upside down, the same notes would, on the contrary, appear to ascend.

Is it not pitiful that, in music, we should be able to quote numerous examples of a form of childishness like this? which is one simply caused by a false interpretation of the terms employed.

The words *ascend* and *descend* are used to express the movement of bodies as they either *increase* or *decrease* their distance from the centre of the earth. I defy anyone to find another sense for these two verbs. Now, how can sound, which is as imponderable as either light or electricity, simply in respect of being more or less grave, either approach or move away from the centre of the earth?

The term "high," or "acute," is applied to the sound produced by a sonorous body in the case of its resulting from a certain *large* number of vibrations in a given time. The term "low" or "grave" is applied in the same way; but the sound in this case is one resulting from a smaller number of vibrations within the same time—vibrations which, therefore, take place more slowly than in the opposite case. The expression "grave" is therefore more suitable than "low," which means nothing. In the same way the term "acute" (as that which pierces the ear, like a sharp or "acute" body) is reasonable, when accepted in the figurative sense; whilst that of "high" cannot fail to be absurd. For why should the product of a string, yielding

thirty-two vibrations

in a second, be any nearer the centre of the earth than the product of another string which, in the same space of time, yields

eight hundred vibrations?

Why should the right-hand side of the keyboard of an organ or piano be called the "top" of it, as is the prevailing custom, when the keyboard itself is horizontal? When a violinist, holding his instrument in the ordinary way, wishes to produce acute sounds, his left-hand in approaching the bridge does certainly rise. But the violoncellist, whose instrument is turned in the contrary direction, is obliged to allow his hand to *descend* in order to produce those very same acute sounds so improperly called "high."

It is, nevertheless, true that this abuse of words, the absurdity of which a moment's attentive examination suffices to expose, is responsible for some of the most inconceivable instances of nonsense; written even by great masters. The natural result has been that people of intelligence, becoming impatient at the aspect of such stupidities, have been led to confound all musical imitations, and to apply the same condemnation to the whole of them. Hence, even those effects which are approved by taste and good sense, and which speak most clearly to the imagination of the listener, have been equally exposed to ridicule.

I well remember the childlike sincerity of a master of composition who desired to hold up to the admiration of his pupil the accompaniment, consisting of descending scales, of a passage in "Alceste," where the high priest, invoking Apollo, the god of day, says:

> Perce d'un rayon éclatant*
> Le voile affreux qui l'environne.

"Do you see," said he, "that scale in demisemi-quavers, perpetually *descending* from C to C in the first violins? That is the *ray*—the brilliant ray, which *descends* at the voice of the high-priest."

But the saddest thing of all to avow is that Gluck really believed that, by doing this, he was somehow imitating the ray.

---

* Pierce with an illuminating ray, etc.

III

"DER FREYSCHÜTZ"

Opera by C. M. von Weber

THE French public now understand and appreciate
this composition, both as a whole and in detail;
although, only a short time ago, it bore the appearance to them of being but an amusing eccen-
tricity. They perceive the reason of what has hitherto
remained obscure, and recognise in Weber the severest
unity of thought, together with the most perfect sentiment of expression. They now see that he combines,
with the dramatic conventions, an abundance of musical ideas; and that he applies this with a most wise
reserve, as well as with an imagination the immense
range of which never lures him beyond the limit where
the ideal finishes and where the absurd begins.

It is, in fact, difficult to find, in either the old or
new school, a score so irreproachable from every point
of view as that of "Der Freyschütz"; so uniformly
interesting from one end to the other; the melody of

which has more freshness in the different forms which it happens to assume; the rhythms of which are more striking; the harmonic inventions of which are more numerous or remarkable; and in which the employment of the vocal and instrumental masses is more energetic without effort or more suave without affectation.

From the commencement of the overture, to the last chord of the final chorus, it seems impossible for me to find a single bar the suppression or alteration of which would be desirable. Intelligence, imagination and genius pervade the whole with such intense brilliancy, that an eagle strength of vision would be necessary not to become fatigued by it; but for the fact that a sensibility, as inexhaustible as it is restrained, is fortunately present to soften the gleam, and to provide listeners with the gentle shelter of its influence.

The overture has now been crowned "queen"; none can be found to contest that fact. It is an overture which now serves as the model of its kind; and the themes, both of its *andante* and *allegro*, are known everywhere. But there is another theme which I am obliged to refer to, because, although it courts less notice, it causes me an incomparably greater emotion than all the rest. I refer to that long plaintive melody, issuing from the clarinet, to a tremolo accompaniment of the stringed instruments; seeming like a distant wail which the winds have dispersed throughout the depths of the woods. It goes straight to the heart; and, in my opinion at any rate, this virginal song, seeming to exhale its timid reproach in a heavenly direction whilst a sombre and threatening harmony trembles beneath it, is one of the newest, the most poetic and the most beautiful contrasts that modern music has produced. In this instrumental inspiration it is already easy to recognise a trace of the character of Agatha; which is soon to develop itself in all its passionate candour. It appertains, however, to the part of Max; being the exclamation of the young hunter at the moment when, from the height of the rocks, he casts his glance into the gulf of the infernal valley. But slightly modified in its outline, and instrumented accordingly, the phrase becomes completely changed in aspect and expression.

It was characteristic of Weber as a composer to possess, in an extreme degree, the art of effecting these melodic transformations.

It would throw upon us the responsibility of writing an entire volume, were we to propose to study separately each one of the traits of this work, so rich in diverse forms of beauty; besides which, so arduous a task could scarcely now be necessary, considering that, by this time, the leading features of its physiognomy are pretty generally known. Everybody admires the satirical gaiety of the couplets of Kilian, with their choral refrain of hearty laughter. There is also the surprising effect of the female voices, combined in major seconds; and the clashing rhythm of the male voices, in completion of this strange concert of jests.

It is impossible not to realise the overwhelming desolation of Max; or the touching generosity breathed by the theme of the chorus which endeavours to console him. Or, again, the exuberant joy of the hardy peasants who are starting for the chase; the comic platitude of the march played by the village fiddlers at the head of Kilian's triumphant procession; and the diabolical song of Gaspard, the mocking laughter of which, as well as the savage clamour of his great air:

Triumph! Triumph!

prepares, in such a threatening way, for the final explosion.

Everybody at present, amateurs and artists alike, listens with delight to that beautiful duet; in which, from the very first, the characters of the two young girls are contrasted. When once this idea of the master has been recognised, no trouble can be experienced in following its development to the end. Agatha is always gentle and meditative. Annette, on the other hand, is the happy child who has not loved; but who takes pleasure in innocent coquetries. Her mirthful chatter and linnet-like song are always appearing to throw sparkling sallies, as it were, right into the midst of the interviews of the two uneasy lovers; always so sadly preoccupied. The listener allows nothing to escape him of the orchestral sighs which go on during the prayer of the young virgin awaiting her lover; or of the rustlings, so sweetly strange, in which an attentive ear seems to recognise:

> Le bruit sourd du noir sapin
> Que le vent des nuits balance.*

It seems, also, as if the obscurity became suddenly more intense and more cold at that magic modulation into C major:

> Tout s'endort dans le silence.†

and, with what a sympathetic emotion we become agitated, later on, at the outburst:

> C'est lui! C'est lui!‡

which, however, cedes in intensity to that immortal cry, shaking our very soul:

> C'est le ciel ouvert pour moi!§

No, no, it must be confessed that there is not another such beautiful air. Never has any master, whether German, French or Italian, produced, in one and the same scene, the full and successive expression of holy prayer, melancholy inquietude, meditation, the repose of nature, the silent eloquence of night, the harmonious mystery of the starlit sky, the torment of waiting, hope, half-certainty, joy, ecstasy, transport and passionate love! And then again what an orchestra he

---

* The dull noise of the black pine waving in the night-wind.
† Everything slumbers in silence.
‡ 'Tis he! 'Tis he!
§ It is heaven open for me.

employs to accompany these noble melodies! What
invention! What ingenious choice of means! What
treasures revealed by a sudden inspiration! The
flutes, in their lower register; the quartet of strings;
the designs in sixths, between violas and violoncellos;
the palpitating rhythm of the basses; the *crescendo*,
which rises and seems to burst at the moment of com-
pleting its luminous ascent; and, finally, the very
silences, during which passion seems to recruit its force,
only to afterwards become aroused to a greater intensity. There is nothing which resembles this in the
pureness of its divine art and poetry and in its realisation of love. If ever Weber heard this scene rendered
in a manner really equal to his dreams, the first occasion of his doing so must have seemed to render all
his later days sad and pale in comparison. He should
have died then; for, what could life have to offer him
after such a joy!

※   ※   ※

Certain theatres in Germany, in order to proceed as
far as possible in the direction of a realism quite opposed to art, have, according to what I hear, employed,
during the scene of casting the balls, some of the most
discordant noises possible; such as cries of animals,
barkings, yelpings, howlings, the breaking of trees,
etc.; but how can the music be heard amidst such a
hideous tumult? And, even in the case of one being
able to hear it, why should the reality be thus placed
side by side with the imitation? If I admire the raw

barking of the horns in the orchestra, that of your theatre-dogs can only inspire me with disgust. The natural cascade, however, is a scenic effect not by any means incompatible with the interest of the score; to which, far from being an injury, it is an addition. The equal and continuous noise of running water conduces to reverie; and is peculiarly impressive during those long organ-points which the composer has so skilfully introduced. It is also an effect which happily combines with the sounds of the distant bell, slowly striking the fatal hour.

When, in 1837 or 1838, there was an intention of producing "Der Freyschütz" at the Opera, it is known that it was I who undertook the task of writing recitatives, in place of the spoken dialogue of the original work; the use of which was forbidden by a regulation of the management. There is no need for me to inform Germans that, in the scene, so strange and bold, that takes place between Samiel and Gaspard, I abstained from giving Samiel anything to sing. There was a formal intention in that; for Weber has allowed Gaspard to sing, but Samiel only to speak the few words of his reply. Once only are the words of the devil rhythmised; each one of his syllables coinciding with a kettle-drum note. The strictness of the rule which forbids the use of spoken dialogue at the Opera does not extend to the exclusion from a musical scene of a few words pronounced in this way; for which reason advantage was taken of the latitude offered, in order to preserve this idea of the composer.

The score of "Der Freyschütz" was, as the result of my perseverance, executed integrally, and in the exact order in which the composer had written it.

The libretto was translated, and not arranged, by M. Emilien Pacini.

The fidelity, too rare at all times and everywhere, with which this masterpiece was then mounted at the Opera caused the finale of the third act to impress the Parisians almost as a novelty. A few had heard it, some fourteen years before, at the summer performances of the German troupe; but the great majority knew nothing of it. This finale is a magnificent conception. Everything sung by Max at the feet of the Prince bears the imprint of repentance and shame. The first chorus, in C minor, after the fall of Agatha and Gaspard, is of beautiful tragic tint; and most suitably announces the catastrophe which is about to take place. Afterwards, we have the return of Agatha to life; her tender exclamation, "Oh, Max!" the *vivats* of the people; the threats of Ottokar and the religious intervention of the hermit. The unction of the latter's conciliatory words; the supplications of all the peasants and hunters to obtain pardon for Max as for a noble heart who has but once gone astray; the sextet, in which hope and happiness are revived; the benediction of the old monk, at which all bow their heads, and which causes to arise from the hearts of the prostrate crowd a hymn so majestic in its brevity; and, finally, the concluding chorus, in which the theme of the *allegro* of the air of Agatha, already heard in the overture, reappears for the third time; all that is beautiful and as worthy of admiration as the preceding— neither more nor less. There is not a note either out of its place or which could be suppressed without injuring the fitness of the whole. Superficial judges will, perhaps, not be of this opinion; but the fact is patent to every attentive listener, and, the more this finale is heard, the stronger becomes the conviction.

A few years after this production of "Der Freyschütz" at the Opera, and whilst I was absent from Paris, Weber's masterpiece was transformed into a curtain-raiser for the ballet; for which purpose it was shortened and mutilated in many ways. The execution, moreover, had become so detestable as to merit being described as scandalous. Will it ever be any better? Let us hope so.

IV

"OBERON"

Opera by C. M. von Weber

Its first representation at the Théâtre-Lyrique, March 6, 1857

THE musical atmosphere of Paris is generally misty, damp, dull and cold—even stormy sometimes; for the seasons there occasionally manifest a strange caprice. At certain moments it snows worms, rains locusts, hails toads; and in such a way that there is no kind of umbrella, whether of cloth or of sheet-iron, capable of protecting honest people from so much vermin. Then, suddenly, the sky becomes clear; it does not rain manna, it is true, but we enjoy a soft and pure air, and are enabled to discover, here and there, some splendid flowers in bloom among the thistles and briars, among the nettles and the spurge; and then it is that we go with delight to scent and gather them.

At the present moment we happen to be in the en-

C

joyment of one of these beneficent beams. Several beautiful flowers of art have just unclosed; and we are still revelling in the fact of having discovered them. Let us first mention the greatest musical event which it has fallen to our lot to signalise for many years; namely, the production of Weber's "Oberon" at the Théâtre-Lyrique. This work, which is a real masterpiece, pure, radiant and complete, has been thirty-one years in existence. It was represented for the first time on April 12, 1826; having been composed by Weber, in Germany, to the words of an English librettist, M. Planchet, at the request of the director of a London lyric theatre; one who believed in the genius of the author of "Der Freyschütz" and who, at the same time, reckoned upon receiving a good score, as well as upon doing some good business.

The principal part (Huon) was written for the celebrated tenor, Braham, who sang it, so they say, with extraordinary verve; a circumstance which did not, however, prevent the new work from suffering an almost complete failure at the hands of the British public. God only knows what was then the degree of musical education of the amateurs on that side of the Channel!

Weber had, in another case, just suffered what may be almost called a defeat in his own country, by the cold reception accorded to "Euryanthe." The public there, whose natural sprightliness is shown by their being capable of swallowing the most frightful ora-

torios; things capable of changing men into stone, or
of freezing spirits of wine; actually thought it the
right thing to get bored with "Euryanthe." Perhaps
they were only too proud to show that their natures
were capable of getting bored at anything, in order
to prove that, after all, their blood did really circulate. That gave them a certain sprightly turn; a gay,
French—even a Parisian air; and, in order to add to
this achievement, they actually invented a pun—or, at
least, what was intended for one, by calling "Euryanthe"—"Ennuyante"—pronouncing the latter expression as "ennyante." To describe the success of
this cumbersome nonsense is impossible, for it still
obtains. For thirty-three years this "joke" has cir-
culated in Germany; and we have still not yet succeeded in persuading these would-be wits that, to call
Euryanthe "Ennuyante," is not good French; and
that, when a piece is tiresome, we call it *ennuyeuse*,
and not *ennuyante*; moreover that even a grocer's as-
sistant in France would be ashamed to commit such a
gross blunder.

For the moment, therefore, "Euryanthe" fell;
crushed by this stupid piece of pleasantry. Sad and
discouraged when asked to write "Oberon," it was
not without hesitation that Weber decided to undertake this new struggle with the public. He resigned
himself to it, however; requesting eighteen months in
order to write his score; by which we see that he did
not reckon upon improvising. Arrived in London, he

had much to contend with at first, on account of the
peculiar ideas of some of his singers; whom, however,
he finally succeeded in bringing to something like
reason. The execution of "Oberon" was satisfactory;
Weber, one of the most skilful conductors of his time,
having been requested to direct it. But the audience
remained cold, serious and dull; "very grave," if I
also may be allowed a play of words which, at any
rate, is English. And so it happened that "Oberon"
made no money; the speculator could not cover his expenses, and, although he had duly received his *good*
score, he had only done very *bad* business. Who can
know what was then passing in the soul of that artist;
he who must have been sure of the value of his work.
In order to encourage him by a success which they
believed was easy to obtain, his friends persuaded him
to give a concert; for which Weber composed a great
cantata, entitled, if I mistake not, the "Triumph of
Peace." The concert took place, the cantata being performed to a nearly empty house, and the receipts not
even covering the expenses.

Weber, on his arrival in London, had accepted the
hospitality of the honourable chapel-master, Sir George
Smart. I do not know whether it happened on returning from this sad concert, or a few days later; but, one
evening, after having chatted for an hour with his
host, Weber retired to bed; and there he was found
by Sir George, the next morning, already cold; his

head resting on one of his hands. He had died from
a rupture of the heart.

Thereupon, a solemn representation of "Oberon"
was announced, all the seats being rapidly sold, the
spectators appearing in mourning, and the house being
full of a select public; whose demeanour seemed to
indicate sincere regret, and the consciousness of their
misfortune at not having sooner understood the work
of one of whom it might be said:

> He was a man, take him for all in all
> We shall not look upon his like again.

* * *

A few months afterwards the overture to "Oberon"
was published; and the Théâtre-de-l'Odéon at Paris,
having scored a great success with their distorted and
crippled version of "Der Freyschütz," were curious to
make the acquaintance at least of something belonging
to Weber's last work. The director ordered this symphonic marvel to be placed in rehearsal; but the orchestra could only discover in it a mere tissue of oddi-
ties, harshness and nonsense; and I am not even aware
if they ever bestowed upon this overture the honour of
strangling it in public.

Ten or twelve years later, those same musicians of
the Odéon, transplanted into the monumental orchestra of the Conservatoire, performed, under competent
direction (that is, under the direction of Habeneck)
this same overture; when they mingled their cries of
admiration with the applause of the public. Eight or

nine years later still, and the society of the Conservatoire concerts performed both a fairy chorus and the
finale to the first act of "Oberon." These were also
acclaimed by the public, with an enthusiasm equal to
that with which they had welcomed the overture. Later
still, two other fragments were produced with equal
success; and that was all.

The next thing was that a little German troupe,
coming to Paris to lose both its time and money during the summer, gave just two performances, about
twenty-seven years ago, of "Oberon" complete. This
took place at the Théâtre-Favart, now called the
Opéra-Comique; the part of Rezia being sung by the
celebrated Madame Schroeder-Devrient. But this
troupe was altogether unsatisfactory; the chorus being
too small and the orchestra miserable. The scenery
was dilapidated and worm-eaten; and the shabbiness
of the costumes even excited pity. Moreover, the more
intelligent section of the musical public were at that
time absent from Paris; so that "Oberon" passed entirely unperceived. A few artists and amateurs more
perspicacious than the rest were the only people who,
in the secrecy of their hearts, adored this divine poem;
applying to Weber the words of Hamlet already
quoted:

> He was a man, take him for all in all
> We shall not look upon his like again.

However, the fact was that, during all this time, Germany had been in enjoyment of the pearl from the British oyster; which the Gallic cock, so partial to grains of millet, had despised. A German translation of M. Planchet's piece gradually spread amongst the theatres of Berlin, Dresden, Hamburg, Leipzig, Frankfort and Munich; so that the score of "Oberon" was saved. I am unaware whether it has been ever performed in its entirety in that intelligent and mischievous city which had found the previous work of Weber "ennyante": * but that is likely enough, for generations follow without resembling each other.

At last, after thirty-one years, chance having placed at the head of one of our lyric theatres in Paris a man who understands and feels music of style; intelligent, bold, active and devoted to the idea which he has once adopted; the marvellous poem of Weber has been revealed to us. The public have not perpetrated any nauseous joke, either upon the master or upon his work; but have applauded it with genuine transports, more and more ardent; and this, notwithstanding that the music disarranges, upsets and generally exhibits a profound disdain of all its habits; even of those which are dearest, most deeply rooted and most inherent to its instincts—either secret or avowed.

The success of "Oberon" at the Théâtre-Lyrique

---

* See also page 19

is very great, very loyal, and very genuine; the audience also being of such good company that the crowd is sure to be attracted. All Paris will want to go and see "Oberon"; to admire its delightful music, its beautiful scenery and rich costumes, and applaud its new tenor. For there is also a tenor who is revealed; M. Carvalho having discovered, for the part of Huon, a true tenor (Michot); and the favour in which this phœnix is held augments at each representation. To complete the explanation of the vogue of this work we may add that, at the conclusion, the laughter is immense; the whole house being in convulsions.

They have not thought it advisable to make a translation, pure and simple, of the libretto of M. Planchet; but a sort of imitation of the latter, and of the poem of "Oberon," by Wieland. I can scarcely estimate whether they have been right or wrong in taking this liberty, but at least the score has been fairly respected. It has been neither mutilated, nor instrumented, nor insulted in any of the usual ways. Certain pieces only have been transplanted from one scene to another; but have always been adapted to a situation similar to that for which they were composed.

The following is the story of this fairy piece. Oberon, the King of the fairies, tenderly loves his Queen, Titania, notwithstanding that the couple frequently quarrel. The cause of this is that Titania persists so obstinately in defending her own sex; probably being mindful of her own strange love for

Bottom, the weaver, a curious character which you can learn all about by reading the "Midsummer Night's Dream," and thus see how far the irony of Shakespeare is ahead of that of the most terrible satirists. On the other hand, Oberon takes likewise the part of his own sex, under all circumstances.

One beautiful summer night he loses patience and separates from Titania, declaring that he will never see her again, except on one condition; and that is, if two young lovers whose mutual affection is pure and abiding show themselves superior to all trials to which their constancy and virtue may be exposed. This is a strange clause: for, after all, whatever high qualities a certain human couple may exhibit can have nothing to do with the bad qualities of Her Fairy Majesty, Queen Titania; and I scarcely see what the King of the fairies can expect to gain in taking back his wife, simply on account of the virtuous triumph of two strangers. Nevertheless, that is the plot of the piece.

Oberon's favourite was a little fairy, very graceful, gently mischievous, frolicsome without being wicked, charming and lovable (at all events, that is the character of Shakespeare's hobgoblin) named Puck. Now, Puck, seeing his master sad and languid, wishes to reunite him to Titania. He makes up his mind upon a plan by which he feels sure to succeed, and immediately sets to work. He has already discovered, at Bordeaux in France, a handsome knight, called Huon;

and, at Bagdad, a charming princess, called Rezia; daughter of the Caliph. By the aid of a dream, which he sends simultaneously to each of them, he causes them to fall in love with one another; and Huon immediately starts off, over the mountains and through the valleys, in search of the princess he adores. A good old woman, whom he meets in the middle of a forest, informs him that Rezia lives at Bagdad; and offers to transport him and his squire Cherasmin in one minute to that place, if Huon will swear to be true to his beloved all his life and patiently await the day of their happy union. Upon Huon pronouncing this double oath, the old woman immediately changes into a pretty fairy; this being simply Puck, resuming his own form. Oberon now comes upon the scene; and, upon his confirming Puck's words, our travellers are immediately transported five hundred leagues away; thus finding themselves in the gardens of the harem of the Caliph of Bagdad.

Rezia is there, deploring the absence of her unknown chevalier; and in despair about an odious marriage, to which her father wishes to compel her. While sauntering in the garden of the palace, she meets the pair who have newly arrived; and in one of whom she recognises the knight of her dreams.

"Oh, happiness! It is then you at last. How I adore you!"

"I come to save you."

"Return at eve; and, when the imam is calling the

believers to prayer, I shall be there; and we can then agree upon everything respecting our flight."

In the evening, accordingly, our lovers meet again; but the palace guards arrest the two strangers, throwing them into prison, and informing the Caliph; who condemns them to death. The supernatural power of Oberon comes to their aid, and they are free. Seizing, by main force, a light ship with which Aboukan (the husband whom the Caliph wished to impose upon Rezia) had come to seek his lady love, they find Rezia; who appears just in the nick of time, with her attendant Fatime, and the whole of the four start off together.

Et vogue la nacelle qui porte leurs amours.*

But, unfortunately, Oberon reads in the heart of the chevalier, and becomes furious at the desires which he there discovers; resolving, on account of them, to separate him from Rezia. He will not allow for the frailty of two lovers such as ours; for their travelling together in a small ship; or for the weariness of a long voyage.

"Blow, tempest, blow! Agitate the ocean, and let the vessel perish!"

The winds accordingly appear. Eurus and Notus and Boreas, and twenty others; followed by the fire spirits, meteors, etc.

---

* God-speed to the skiff which carries their love.

Black night extends over the waters. Rezia is
thrown, alone, upon a rock; whilst another reef re-
ceives Fatime and Cherasmin; the fate of Huon remaining unknown. Shipwreck is not to be the end of
their troubles, however; for they are taken by bar-
barous pirates, and, being conducted to the coast of
Africa, are sold to the Bey of Tunis. Rezia is exposed to the honours of the harem, having inspired a
violent passion in the Bey. The two other lovers (for
Cherasmin and Fatime have also wound up by loving
one another most tenderly) are more happy, as they
are not separated; their task as slaves being also light,
as they have merely to cultivate one of the gardens of
his highness.

They are informed, by the eunuch, Aboulifar, of
a revolution which is about to take place in the harem,
and which is to consist of the deposition of the
former favourite and the elevation of Rezia.

But Rezia repulses, with disdain, the homage of the
Bey; being resolved to remain faithful unto death to
her beloved knight. Puck, skilfully turning this noble
constancy to good account, persuades Oberon to grant
Huon a last and solemn test; in order that he may
be enabled to prove himself worthy of favour. To
this the fairy King consents; and Puck, losing no time
in discovering Huon, transports him into the garden
of the Bey of Tunis. There, we see him surrounded
by a crowd of houris, each vieing with the other for
beauty; and who dance and sing, and fold him in their

arms, caress him with their glances, and devour him
with smiles; but all in vain. Huon remains firm
against all forms of seduction; for he loves Rezia, and
Rezia alone, and to her he is resolved to remain faithful. Suddenly, the Bey appears; and, finding a
stranger in the midst of his wives, orders his immedi-
ate impalement. His execution is about to be proceeded with, but the test of both lovers has now proved
decisive; love has triumphed, and Oberon is satisfied.
His enchanted horn is heard; and at once the Bey,
the chief of the eunuchs, the guards of the harem, and
the whole harem itself, yield to an irresistible impulse
obliging them to dance; to turn round and round like
the dervishes, and to continue whirling; keeping up
the one rotary motion, which, under the lively, imperi-
ous and pitiless influence of Oberon's magic horn,
becomes more and more rapid; until, on a stroke of
the tam-tam, the whole crowd fall to the ground in a
dazed condition, and half dead. Thereupon, Oberon,
together with his beautiful Titania and faithful Puck,
rise to heaven in a glory; but, before doing so, the
fairy King addresses the lovers in these words :

"You have remained faithful one to another, and
have patiently awaited your time of union; now be
happy! Return to France; and you, Huon, present
yourself at the court of France; my protection will
follow you."

It would be necessary to write at considerable length,
worthily to analyse the score of "Oberon"; to examine

the questions to which the style of the work gives rise, to explain the various modes of procedure adopted by the composer, and to discover the cause of the delight which this music affords to all listeners; not merely including those devoid of intellectual training, but also those who even lack sentiment for the art of sounds.

"Oberon" is the counterpart of "Der Freyschütz"; one combining the fantastic with what is sombre, violent and diabolical; the other applying it to the domain of fairy-land, and therefore combining it with smiles, grace and enchantment. The supernatural is so happily combined with the actual world in this piece that it is difficult to make out precisely where one ends, and where the other begins. Passion and sentiment are also expressed in it, by language and accents which always produce the impression of never having been heard before.

This music is essentially melodious, though in quite a different way from that of the greatest melodists. Its melody seems to be exhaled from the voices and instruments; like a subtle perfume which spreads a sensation of enjoyment, the precise nature of which we cannot, at first, determine. A phrase, the commencement of which has not been noticed, is already mistress of the situation when we first observe it; whilst another, the disappearance of which has not been remarked, continues to preoccupy us some time after it has ceased to remain audible. The principal

charm is that of grace—in a form which, though exquisite, is somewhat strange; so that Weber's inspiration in "Oberon" might fitly be described in the
words which Laërtes applies to his sister, Ophelia:

> Thought and affliction; passion, hell itself,
> She turns to favour and to prettiness,

but that hell does not figure in it. Besides that, however, the subject of hell is one which Weber never seeks
to soften; giving it, on the contrary, most frightful
and terrible forms.

The harmonic progressions of Weber have a colour
not to be found in any other master; and one reflecting
more upon the melody than we are liable to suppose.
The effect is due sometimes to an alteration of certain
notes of the chord, sometimes to the employment of
unusual inversions, and sometimes even to the suppression of particular sounds generally held to be indispensable. A case of this kind occurs at the final
chord of the piece given to the nymphs of the sea;
where the tonic is suppressed, and in which, although
the piece is in E, the composer has only allowed G
sharp and B to be heard. Hence the vagueness of
this termination, and its effect of dreaminess upon
the listener.

Almost the same may be said of his modulations;
for, however strange they may be, they are always
artistically introduced, without harshness or shock.
At the same time, they are nearly always unexpected;

being employed to assist an expression of sentiment, and not to cause the ear a mere puerile surprise.

Weber admits an absolute liberty of rhythmic form. No composer has ever more completely freed himself from the tyranny of what is called the *carrure*; the exclusive application of which to agglomerations of even numbers contributes so cruelly, not only to cause monotony, but to produce actual platitude. In "Der Freyschütz" he already gave numerous examples of a new phraseology; some of these being so striking that French musicians, who are the "squarest" of all melodists (after the Italians), were quite surprised to applaud, for example, the drinking-song of Gaspard; this being composed, as to its first part, of a succession of three-bar phrases—the second being an ordinary succession of those of four bars. In "Oberon" several passages occur in which the melodic texture is rhythmised in five-bar phrases. Generally speaking, each phrase, either of five or three bars, has its counterpart; thus constituting symmetry by producing an even number, and giving the duple character so dear to vulgar musicians, in spite of the proverb:

Numero Deus impare gaudet.

But Weber did not regard himself as obliged to establish this symmetry always and at any price; and, accordingly, we often find his phrase consisting of an odd number of bars, unprovided with pendant. I appeal to men of letters, whether La Fontaine has not employed an excellent form, in casting a little isolated line of two feet at the end of one of his fables:

> Mais qu'en sort-il souvent?
> Du vent.

Their affirmative reply, which I may confidently assume, justifies the analogous procedure applied musically by many masters; amongst whom may be cited Weber, Gluck and Beethoven. It is, in fact, just as absurd to endeavour to rhythmise music exclusively from four to four bars as only to admit into poetry a single kind of verse.

If, instead of having so beautifully said:

> Mais qu'en sort-il souvent?
> Du vent.*

the fabulist had written:

> Mais qu'en sort-il souvent?
> Il n'en sort que du vent.†

he would have terminated his fable by an insupportable platitude. The analogy of this example with the musical question upon which we are engaged is so striking, that nothing but the obstinacy of routine could fail to recognise it, or could deny its consequences.

But if, on the one hand, it appears evident to us that

---

* But, issuing thence, what do we find?
But wind.

† But, issuing thence, what do we find?
There simply issues naught but wind.

D

music neither can nor ought to conform itself blindly
to the usage of certain schools which aim at preserving
the squarest of squareness under all circumstances; if
we find, in this ridiculous obstinacy in maintaining a
prejudice, the cause of the insipidity, baseness of style
and exasperating vulgarity of a crowd of productions
of all periods and of all countries; it is no less clear
to us, on the other hand, that certain irregularities exist, which are of such disturbing character as to require
to be avoided with the greatest care.   Gluck has committed a great number of them, and especially in his
"Iphigenia in Aulide," faults which, it must be confessed, injure the feeling for rhythmic harmony.
Weber is not exempt from them; and there is even a
very regrettable example in one of the most delightful
pieces of "Oberon"—the song of Naiades, which I
spoke of just now.   After the first vocal period, composed of four times four bars, the composer wished to
give the voice a short repose.   Thinking, no doubt, that
no account would be taken of the instrumental frag-
ment, the author has, afterwards, resumed his vocal
song with a square rhythm; as if the orchestral bar
had not existed.   In our opinion he made a mistake.
The ear suffers by this addition of a bar to the vocal
phrase.   It perfectly perceives that the movement of
oscillation has been broken; and that the phrase has
lost the regularity of balance which gave it so much
charm.   Returning to my comparison of melody with
versification, I may say that, in the case in question,

the defect is of the same nature as would appear in a verse consisting of lines of ten feet, if one of them were allowed to have eleven.

Of the instrumentation of Weber I need only say that it is of a richness, variety and novelty, altogether admirable. That distinction is its dominating quality is shown by an absence of all means disclaimed by good taste; as well as of all coarseness and absurdity. Everywhere, there is a charming colouring, and a sonority full of life, but harmonious. There is also evidence of a strength which is restrained, and of profound acquaintance with the nature of each instrument, with its characteristics, and with both its sympathies and antipathies, as regards other members of the orchestral family. There is also, everywhere preserved, an intimate relation between the theatre and the orchestra; no effect being introduced without direct object, nor any accent without motive.

Weber is reproached for his style of vocal writing; and, unfortunately, such blame is well founded. He often imposes upon the voice successions of excessive difficulty, such as could be comfortably executed upon no instrument except the piano. But this defect, which does not extend so far as some are inclined to make out, ceases to remain one where strangeness of vocal design is directly caused by a dramatic intention. It is then, on the contrary, a good quality; the author only remaining blameable in the estimation of singers, who are discontented at being obliged to take pains, and engage in studies which conventional music does not impose upon them.

Of this description are certain truly diabolical passages of the part of Gaspard, in "Der Freyschütz"; passages which, in my opinion, are evident traits of genius.

Out of the twenty pieces of which the score of "Oberon" is composed there is not one that can be described as weak. Invention, inspiration, knowledge and good sense are conspicuous in all of them. It is, therefore, almost with regret that the following pieces are to be mentioned as preferable to the others.

They are :

1. The mysterious and suave chorus of the introduction, sung by the fairies round the bed of flowers on which Oberon is sleeping.

2. The knightly song of Huon, in which occurs a delightful phrase already presented in the middle of the overture.

3. The marvellous nocturnal march of the guards of the seraglio, which terminates the first act.

4. The chorus, so energetic and sharply characterised, entitled :

Gloire au chef des croyants !

5. The prayer of Huon, accompanied only by violas, violoncellos and basses.

6. The dramatic scene of Rezia on the seashore.

7. The song of the nymphs.

(This is now confided to Puck in the new version of the libretto; but wrongly so, as I consider. It ought to be sung from the back of the stage, on one of the portions of the sea-scenery, by several voices in unison, and with extreme softness.)

8. The fairy choral-dance, which concludes the second act.

9. The air, so gracefully gay, of Fatime; as well as the duet which follows it, with its ostenato orchestral trait, returning at irregular intervals.

10. The trio, which is so harmonious and admirably modulated, and which is accompanied *pianissimo* by the brass; and, finally—

11. The choral-dance in the scene of the houris; a piece quite unique in its way. Never has melody been invested with such smiling rhythm, or with more irresistible caresses. It seems as if nothing could have enabled Huon to escape the allurements of women singing such melodies, short of having virtue absolutely *rivetted* into his body.

The audience demanded the repetition of four numbers besides the overture; and the crowd, who for three hours had enjoyed this music of so new a flavour, departed in a mental condition of delightful excitement. It was indeed a success; a noble and great success.

The tenor, Michot, is gifted with a beautiful voice, of rich and sympathetic timbre, which study will not fail to render more flexible. Every night he is recalled, and may now be considered *posé*, as they say in the theatres. He will become, and in fact is already, an important personage. Madame Rossi-Caccia, after a long absence from the theatre, reappeared in the difficult part of Rezia; which she sings with talent. Mademoiselle Girard makes an excellent Fatime. But why can she not correct the trembling of her voice? Mademoiselle Borghèse sings and plays well the part of Puck, the hobgoblin; only she is too tall—for which, however, we shall not find fault with her. Grillon acquits himself well in the part of Cherasmin; and Fromant, in that of Oberon. As to the eunuch, Girardot, he excites hilarity by his costume, his attitudes, his strange voice and his jokes.

Being desirous of reproducing the masterpiece of Weber without meanness, M. Carvalho added ten strings to the orchestra; which he could only do by encroaching upon the public seats. He also enriched the fairy chorus by twelve female voices. The general style of production was, moreover, well thought out in every detail; the effect of the apotheosis of Titania and Oberon being exceptionally poetical.

V

"ABU-HASSAN"

OPERA, IN ONE ACT, BY THE YOUNG WEBER

AND

"IL SERAGLIO"

OPERA, IN TWO ACTS, BY THE YOUNG MOZART

Their first representation at the Théâtre-Lyrique, May 19, 1859

ABU-HASSAN is a peculiar kind of Turk in love; whose head is inferior to his heart, as they say, besides which he has made some debts. They give him money; but, instead of using it to satisfy his creditors, he buys presents for his lady-love; and, when the time comes for payment, there is nothing left.

Now his master, the Pasha, is accustomed to give one thousand piastres (I am not quite sure of the kind of money) upon the occasion of the funeral of each of his servants; so Abu-Hassan conceives the idea of counterfeiting death. His lady-love (it might even have been his wife) rivals him in zeal to the extent of counterfeiting death also. In this way, the Pasha will naturally have to part with *two* thousand piastres; a sum which the lovers calculate will comfortably get them out of trouble. But the Pasha discovers the ruse; though, as he laughs at it, his anger is disarmed, and he has to forgive. Thus, the couple come to life again, and everyone is pleased.

Weber was seventeen years old when he wrote the score of this ingenious piece. They even say that M. Meyerbeer aided him somewhat in the work. But Meyerbeer himself was only sixteen and a half years old at that time; so that the author of the "Huguenots" is now absolutely unable to recognise the pieces with which he ornamented the work of his friend. Thus, if any old bibliophile were to come to him and say positively:

"This is your melody"—

he would be in a position to give him the same answer as good La Fontaine once gave, when they pointed out a young man to him as his son:

"That is very possible!"

Thus it is that the score of "Abu-Hassan" naturally contains several juvenile curiosities of rather good form; and, amongst others, an air which Meillet sang splendidly and which was redemanded with great acclamation. Meillet, moreover, plays his entire part with zest and verve; keeping well within the bounds of good taste. His success was complete, both as actor and singer.

The opera of "Il Seraglio" is much older than that

of "Abu-Hassan"; and probably Mozart, when he wrote it, was not even seventeen years old. Anyone desirous of knowing precisely how the case stands can consult the book of M. Oulibicheff. This Russian knew the precise hour at which the author of "Don Giovanni" wrote the last note of every one of his sonatas for the clavichord. He knew who fainted on hearing two clarinets play a major third in the orchestra of Mozart's first opera; and who was angry if the two clarinets played the same notes in Beethoven's "Fidelio." M. Oulibicheff is only doubtful upon one point; and that is he was not quite sure whether Mozart was God.

"Il Seraglio" is preceded by a little overture in C; a piece of the utmost simplicity, producing little sensation, and probably not being even noticed by the pit. Without offence, let this be recorded to the pit's credit; for, really, if it is permissible to speak the truth about it, old father Leopold Mozart, instead of weeping with admiration as usual before this work of his son, would have done better to burn it, and to say to the young composer:

"My boy, you have just turned out a most ridiculous overture. I daresay you said your rosary before you started; but you will have to write another one all the same; and you had better say your rosary, this time, expressly to ask the saints to give you a better inspiration."

"Nonsense! abominable! blasphemous!" all the followers of Oulibicheff will cry; rending their garments and covering their heads with ashes.

Come, calm yourselves! most venerable men; and also spare your garments. "Use powder for your heads instead of ashes; for our opinion bears no trace of blasphemy. It nowadays is quite well proved that, at the age of fifteen years, Mozart was not quite God. Know ye, moreover, that our praise is stronger far than yours; that we know him better far than you; and that our admiration is but deeper for the very reason that it does not result from foolish love or prejudice which is absurd.

The book of "Il Seraglio" is on another Turkish subject; and introduces the inevitable European slave who resists the equally inevitable Pasha. This slave has a pretty companion, and each of the pair has a lover. The two swains in question expose themselves to the danger of being impaled, through an attempt to deliver their beauties from captivity. They succeed in getting into the seraglio, bringing with them a ladder; not to say, two ladders.

But Osmin, a hateful Turk, though unfortunately in the Pasha's confidence, defeats their project, carries off one of the ladders, arrests the whole party, and is about to give them over for impalement—when the Pasha appears. The latter is only a sham Turk, of Spanish origin; and when he learns that Belmont, the lover of Constance, is the son of one of his Spanish friends, a man who formerly saved his life, he hastens to deliver the whole of the lovers and to send them back to Europe; where they probably, afterwards, had many children.

Now you know the strength of the libretto; and it would be stronger still for me to say that Mozart had written anything approaching a marvel of inspiration upon it. There are many pretty vocal pieces, no doubt; but also many formulas, all the more to be regretted, not only on account of Mozart having employed them later in his masterpieces, but also because, nowadays, they are a positive nuisance.

Generally speaking, the melody of this opera is simple, sweet and not very original; being provided with accompaniments which are discreet, agreeable, but slightly varied, and childish. The instrumentation is simply that of the period; but already better disposed than in the works of the author's contemporaries. The score contains frequent instances of what then went by the name of "Turkish music"; consisting of bass-drum, cymbals and triangle, employed in an altogether primitive manner. Besides that, Mozart has used a small "fifth" flute in G (called "in A," at the period when ordinary flutes were considered as being in D); and he sometimes formed a trio by using this G instrument with the two large flutes.

If the first air of Osmin bore the name of any living composer, we should be justified in finding it altogether deprived of interest; and, if the three verses, afterwards sung by the same character, had been re-

garded in this way, they certainly would not have had
to be repeated. The chorus, with accompaniment of
Turkish music, is characteristic. The duet, in $\frac{6}{8}$ time
between Osmin and the companion is poorly col-
oured, is not striking, contains many high notes which
the soprano can only venture upon at her risk and
peril, and is altogether of a most inferior effect. The
allegro of the air which follows offers an unfortunate
resemblance with the popular Parisian tune :

En avant, Fanfan la Tulipe !

which Mozart most certainly never knew. We must
therefore remodel the phrase, convert blame into
praise, and say : the popular Parisian "pont-neuf"
tune has the honour of resembling the theme of an
allegro by Mozart.

The air of Belmont, on the contrary, is melodious,
expressive and charming. The quartet, which is of
extreme simplicity, assumes a certain animation
towards the coda; thanks to the intervention of a rapid
violin passage. A march, with mutes, well concludes
the first act.

The air of the soubrette is, unfortunately, disfigured
by the grotesque passages and vocalisations habitually
employed by Mozart, even in his most magnificent
works. It was the taste of the period, perhaps; but so
much the worse for the period, and so much the worse
for us now. Mozart would certainly have done better
to have consulted his own taste. The soprano part of

this piece is, moreover, written constantly in the upper register; a defect probably less felt when the pitch was at least a semitone lower than it is at present.

The humorous verses, sung by Bataille and Froment were honoured by a recall. The air in D, of Osmin, which succeeded them, presents the peculiarity, exceptional in Mozart, of a theme in three-bar phrases, followed by those of four bars. Even Mozart appears, therefore, not to have thought it mad to rhythmise a melody otherwise than in "square" form. An entire system is upset by that fact.

The part of Belmont contains also a graceful romance, and the song of the signal, with its accompaniment for strings in pizzicato, is piquant. But, in my view, the best piece of the whole score is the duet between Constance and Belmont, with which it concludes. The sentiment is very fine; the style much more elevated than all the preceding; the form is broader; and the ideas are developed in a more masterly way.

"Il Seraglio," according to all our critical colleagues, was treated at the Théâtre-Lyrique with *scrupulous fidelity.* This means that all they did was:

1. To invert the order of succession of several numbers.

2. To take out a grand air from the part of Madame Meillet, and insert it into that of Madame Ugalde;

3. To play, between their *two* acts, the famous Turkish march, so well known to pianists; and—

4. To render in *two* acts what had been written for *three*.

Well! well! not so bad for what they call a *scrupulous fidelity*.

VI

ON THE MEANS DISCOVERED BY M. DEL-SARTE FOR TUNING STRINGED INSTRUMENTS

Without the Aid of the Ear

DO you realise this?—all you pianists; guitarists; violinists; violoncellists; contra-bassists; harpists; and you, too, conductors!

Without the help of the ear!!!

The discovery is immense; incomparable; and, especially for us poor listeners, who now have sadly to tolerate so many discordant pianos, violins and 'cellos; discordant harps and orchestras. M. Delsarte's invention places upon you the obligation of not torturing us any more; and of no longer making us perspire with pain, and harbour thoughts of suicide.

Without the help of the ear!!!

By means of this invention, not only does the ear

become useless for tuning purposes, and dangerous to consult; but it must absolutely *not* be consulted. Think of the advantage for those who have not any! Until now, the contrary was the case; and accordingly we pardoned you all the torments you inflicted. But, in future, if your instruments or orchestras are not in tune, you will have no excuse; and we shall give you over to public vengeance.

Without the help of the ear!!!

Help so often useless, deceptive and fatal. The discovery of M. Delsarte only applies to stringed instruments; but that is much, in fact, enormous; for hence it follows that, in orchestras directed and tuned in this way, there will be no more discordance except amongst flutes, oboes, clarinets, bassoons, horns, cornets, trumpets, trombones, the ophicleide, the tuba and the kettle-drums. The triangle might, as an extreme case, be tuned in the new manner; but it is generally recognised that that is not necessary, for, in common with the bells, the discordance between the triangle and other instruments *does good*; and they quite like it in all lyric theatres.

And the singers? You do not speak of them, it may be said. Will it be possible to make them sing in tune? to make them tune themselves?

The singers? Why two or three of them are naturally in tune. And a few others, perhaps, by dint of great care and strictness, might be nearly tuned. But all the rest never were, never are, and never will be, in tune; neither individually, nor amongst themselves, nor with the instruments, nor with the conductor, nor with the rhythm, nor with the harmony, nor with the accent, nor with the expression, nor with the pitch, nor with the language, nor with anything that resembles precision or good sense. For some time now they have not been even in tune with the claqueurs; who threaten to give them up. That will be all very well; but what an unfortunate thing!

M. Delsarte has rendered the tuning especially of the piano easily practicable by means of an instrument which he calls the—

"Phonoptique";

the description of which would be too lengthy to give in this place. It will suffice to say that it contains a needle indicating the precise moment when two or more strings are exactly in unison, to which may be added that the invariable result of the operation is, for whoever will take the trouble, an accuracy with which the most practised ear cannot compete.

Professors of acoustics will not fail to occupy themselves, before long, with the valuable invention referred to; the use of which cannot possibly fail to become popular.

E

VII

THE TREATISE ON CHURCH MUSIC
BY M. JOSEPH D'ORTIGUE

THE author of the above work possesses the literary probity, as also the modesty now so rare, of
declaring in his preface that he presents us with
a volume—and not a book. "It is," he says, "a collection of articles relating to plain-chant and church
music; published in the journals and reviews, at various times during the last twenty-five years. These
articles, between the writing of which very often a
long time elapsed, were disseminated here and there
in the pages of various publications, differing greatly
from one another in tendency and spirit. They were
thus in the first place addressed to many kinds of
readers. But now, having been subjected to a complete revision, some having been entirely re-written,
they may, as thus formed into a collection, be almost
regarded as seeing the light of day for the first time.
Such is this volume; which, in point of material is

old, but which, in its entirety, may possibly be regarded as presenting some novelty.

It does, in fact, present very great novelty; besides adding to that attraction the special interest possessed by all useful books; and especially when they are written in a style which is elegant, correct and perfectly clear. The latter quality is for many persons, of whom I am one, of considerable value; nothing being more odious to them than that ambiguous style, the pretended depth of which is designed not so much for the purpose of veiling the author's thought, and of rendering its perception difficult, as to conceal the fact that he has no thought worth mentioning. The reader generally shuts a book of this kind at about the fourth page, saying; "I cannot see what the writer meant, and possibly he did not know it himself." This reflection, by the way, recalls to me a treatise on harmony; composed according to a most ingenious system, I was told, by a most learned mathematician.

Now, I read this treatise with an attention which nearly made me ill, without understanding the least bit about it; but the author, to whom I confessed that the sense of his work escaped me completely, kindly offered to come and explain it. We had a long interview on the subject; but the verbal explanations no more succeeded than the written prose had done, in penetrating me with the meaning of the mysterious treatise.

"I fear I am not very well disposed to-day," said I to the author. "If you would kindly grant me another occasion, I should hope to be more intelligent at a second trial." We had another meeting for I had, by this time, become genuinely curious to see if I could not succeed in understanding it. The theorist returned; renewing the exposition of his doctrine, of his examples, and of his system, in detail. I made superhuman efforts of attention, at which my brain seemed to reel; whilst the author was quite in a perspiration, at the aspect of so much good-will, without any result. At last, I was obliged to renounce the attempt, and to say to the demonstrator: "It is useless, my dear sir, for I have not the least idea of what you wish to make me understand. It is precisely as if you spoke to me in Chinese." And this learned man had, nevertheless, written a great book in order to teach harmony *to those who did not know it!*

Nothing of this kind, I may repeat, is to be found in the work of M. d'Ortigue; and, if I differ in opinion from him on certain points, at least I know what the difference is, and why it exists. The principal object of his work is to study and to render intelligible the nature of religious musical art; that is to say, of the art of sounds applied to the service of religion, and to the singing of the sacred texts in Catholic churches. Also, to demonstrate the aberrations of musicians who have undertaken this task without appreciating its importance; as well as to point out the culpable tolerance of the clergy in their respect—a tolerance only to be explained by profound ignorance of the expressive aspect of musical art, and by absence of taste. The work of M. d'Ortigue proposes, moreover, to exalt the musical system of plain-chant at the expense of modern music; that is, at the expense of music proper, by declaring that plain-chant alone is capable of worthily expressing religious sentiment. Consequently, the author seeks, on the one hand, the means of remedying innumerable abuses of music introduced to the Church; and, on the other, those of extricating plain-chant from the corruption into which it has fallen.

These revolting abuses of which he gives examples are, it is true, not peculiar to our time. It is well known to what a degree of cynicism and imbecility the ancient contrapuntists went; in taking, for their so-called "religious" compositions, the themes of popular songs. The words of the latter were jovial, occasionally obscene, besides being universally known; yet, they made them serve as the foundation of their harmonic plot during divine service. Of this kind of work the mass called "L'homme armé," is a familiar example. It is precisely in the destruction of this barbarism that the glory of Palestrina consists.

We have nevertheless seen, scarcely as far back as thirty years ago, what our missionary priests were capable of; with their stupid affection for music, coupled with a zeal both blind and deaf. In the church of Sainte-Geneviève, during the ceremonies, they actually caused hymns to be sung, the melodies for which had been taken from vaudevilles of the Theatre of·Varieties; such as the following:

> C'est l'amour, l'amour, l'amour,*
> Qui fait le monde
> A la ronde !

But the masterpiece of this kind of thing has been more recently furnished by a musician of a certain notoriety, who has actually dared to print it for the edification of religious souls and people of good sense. This is not a made-up tale; for I have read the monstrous production. This is how M. d'Ortigue speaks about it:

I have said, in a preceding article, that the "Concerts Spirituels," published at Avignon in 1835, had been surpassed by a still stranger production. They have indeed been surpassed; and, to a great extent, in the work entitled

"Mass by Rossini,"

published a few years ago by this witty, but too jovial, Castil-Blaze; who seemed desirous of setting a crown to his career as an arranger, by an "arrangement" of the most unheard-of description which could well be imagined—quite as if his intention had been to offer a challenge to himself.

All I shall do will be to indicate the principal items of this "Rossini Mass." The "Kyrie" is the entrance-march from "Othello." The "Gloria" begins with the opening chorus of the same work; which also furnishes some other fragments, up to the second half of the final "verset"—

"Cum Sancto Spiritu, in gloria Dei patris: Amen,"

---

* 'Tis love that makes the world go round.

the words of which the arranger has adjusted to the stretto
of "Cenerentola," a comic item of reckless gaiety, in quick
allegro and triple-time. It is almost impossible to realise the
extravagant and grotesque effect of the text—

" Cum Sanctu Spiritu,"

given out, syllable by syllable, to quavers with an accellerated
movement.

The remainder is all of the same sort. The "Credo" opens
with the romance from the "Barber of Seville," called "Ecco
ridente il cielo"; then come the warlike duets from "Tancredi" and from "Othello." The "Resurrexit" is set to
roulades, with extensive ramifications, and finally the "Et
vitam venturi seculi" is on the motive of Arsace from the
finale of "Semiramide," "Atro evento prodigio."

One word more. The "Dona nobis pacem" is hammered
out in repeated chords by the chorus to a "cabalette" from
"Tancredi," as pretty and fanciful a piece as could anywhere
be found.

It need scarcely be said that M. d'Ortigue does not
make Rossini responsible for all this extravagance,
and that his censure applies to the arranger alone.
But he blames the illustrious master very greatly for
certain parts of his "Stabat Mater"; and he rightly
considers this work, on the whole, to be more theatrical than religious. But this is not the fault of music,
or of "mundane" art, as he calls it; and he is wrong
to allow himself gradually to be drawn into making
this beautiful art responsible for the errors of musicians, and, in this direction, to go so far as to declare
that there *cannot exist any true religious music outside
the ecclesiastical tones.*

According to this, the "Ave Verum," of Mozart, that
sublime expression of ecstatic adoration, which is not

written to any ecclesiastical tone, is not to be considered as true religious music. Here it is that M. d'Ortigue evinces a partiality for plain-chant which, we confess, we do not share. Moreover, it is impossible for us to understand why this plain-chant, of Greek and pagan origin, should be considered worthy to sing the praises of the God of the Christians; and yet, at the same time, *music proper* (which is a modern art, discovered by the Christians themselves with riches of many kinds of which plain-chant is entirely destitute) is not to be thought fit for that purpose.

It is precisely the simplicity, the vagueness, the uncertain tonality, the want of expression—in a word—the *impersonality* of plain-chant which is its principal merit in the eyes of M. d'Ortigue. It seems to me that a statue reciting the liturgical words with a cold impassibility upon a single note should realise M. d'Ortigue's ideal of religious music. He does not go so far as that; although that is the conclusion to which his theory should lead him.

What he censures most is the manner in which plain-chant is usually performed; this amounting to its being bellowed, or roared in bull-fashion to an accompaniment of serpent or ophicleide. He is certainly quite right. To hear such successions of hideous notes, with threatening accents, one might imagine themselves transported to a cave of Druids at the moment of their preparing for a human sacrifice. This is frightful, though I must admit that every piece of plain-chant

I have heard was so performed, and might fairly be described in this way.

An exhaustive discussion upon this subject and kindred questions would lead us very far; but I think it would be easy, whilst sharing the indignation of our learned colleague and friend against the abuses which have been introduced into church music, and against the revolting errors into which *nearly all* great masters have fallen in treating this difficult style, I think, I say, that it would be easy to rehabilitate real music. Music itself is not guilty of the bad use which is made of its power and riches. It is, moreover, capable of producing all effects of plain-chant at pleasure; whilst plain-chant, on the other hand, must forcibly remain powerless to produce the effects of modern music. But, however this may be, it is our duty to give much praise to this book about church music; and to recommend it to all readers who are interested in the dignity both of divine worship and of art. Members of the clergy especially who, in virtue of their position are bound to exercise a direct influence on the musical dispositions of their churches, can only gain by meditating upon its contents.

Nocturna versate manu, versate diurna.

VIII

CHINESE MUSICAL MANNERS

WE have been busy about China for some time; but this always happens in a way which is not very flattering for the natives of that country. We are not contented with beating them, and with upsetting everything in their shops; with putting their Emperor to flight, and with taking possession of his celestial majesty's palace; as well as with seizing his ingots, his diamonds, precious stones and silks; and sharing them out amongst ourselves; but we must also make fun of this great people, designating them as a nation of maniacs, fools and imbeciles; as lovers of the absurd, the horrible and the grotesque. We laugh at their beliefs and at their manners; at their arts and at their science; even their familiar customs do not escape. Our excuse for this last form of derision is that the Chinaman eats his rice, grain by grain, with chop-sticks; and that he takes as long to learn how to use these ridiculous utensils as to learn to write (a thing, by the way, which he never does learn, completely) just as if, we are inclined to say, it were not much easier to eat rice with a spoon!

We laugh at his arms too, and at his armies; at his standards, with dragons painted upon them in order to frighten the enemy, and at his old tinder guns and his cannons with bullets to reach the moon. Then, there are his musical instruments; and his women with distorted feet—everything affords us cause for laughter.

For all that, there is good in the Chinese people—much good; and it is not altogether without reason that he calls us (that is to say, all Europeans) red devils and barbarians. For instance, sixty thousand Chinese are completely routed by four or five thousand Anglo-French, it is true; but their General, seeing the battle lost, cuts his throat with his own sabre without having recourse to the help of his servant for that purpose—as the Romans did. Nor is he satisfied until his head has fallen. That is courageous; see if you can do it.

He crushes the feet of his women in such a way as to prevent them from walking. But the very same plan prevents them even more effectively from going to the ball and from dancing the polka; from waltzing and consequently from remaining the entire night on the arms of young men who squeeze their waist, clasp them tightly, and whisper into their ear—under the very eyes of their fathers, mothers, husbands and lovers.

We find his music abominable; atrocious; and that he sings like the dogs yawn; or like the cats behave when they have swallowed a fish-bone. The instruments, also, which he employs to accompany the foregoing, strike us as being real instruments of torture. But, at least, he respects his music, such as it is; and he protects the remarkable works which Chinese genius has produced; whilst we have no more protection for our masterpieces than horror for our abominations; both being equally left to take their chance with an indifferent public.

The Chinese regulate everything by an immutable code, even to the instrumentation of operas. The size of the tamtams and the gongs is determined according to the subject of the drama, and the musical style which is suitable to it. It is not permitted to employ, for a comic-opera, tamtams as large as for a more serious work. With us, on the contrary, the bass-drums in use for the slightest lyric trifle are as large as those employed for the grand opera. This was not the case five and twenty years ago; which is another proof of the advantages of the immutability of the Chinese musical code.

Notwithstanding the disastrous results of our changeful and unregulated manners, our music has, nevertheless, the advantage, in certain respects, over that of the inhabitants of the Celestial Empire. Thus,

according to the avowal of the mandarin-directors of
melody themselves, Chinese singers are often out of
tune; which proves how inferior they are to ours, whose
intonation is so often good. But nearly all Chinese
singers know their language; observing its prosidy,
and not violating its accentuation. Five and twenty
years ago it was the same with us; but now, as a result
of our mania for upsetting things, by taking notice of
everybody's caprice, the majority of European singers
seem as if they were singing in Chinese.

What is truly beautiful, and worthy of admiration
on our part is the regulation, afforded by the law in
force in the Celestial Empire, of means for the protection of the masterpieces of composers. It is not permitted to disfigure them, to interpret them unfaith-
fully, or to alter either their text, sentiment or spirit.
These laws are not preventive; and they restrict no
one from attempting the execution of a consecrated
work. But the individual convicted of having disfigured it is punished, more or less severely, in the
same degree as the author is more or less illustrious
and admired. Thus, the penalties incurred by those
who profane the works of Confucius appear cruel to
barbarians like ourselves, accustomed to outrage everything with impunity. This Confucius is called by the
Chinese Koang-fu-tsee; which exemplifies the pretty
habit we have of *arranging* proper names, just like we
arrange works when we translate them from one language to another, or when we take them simply from

one scene to another scene. We are equally unable to preserve integrally the names of the great men and those of the great cities of foreign nations. In France, we give the name of Ratisbonne to the German town which the Germans themselves call Regensburg; and the Italians call Paris by the name of Parigi. This added syllable *gi* (pronounced *d gi*) pleases them immensely; and their ear would be quite shocked if they said Paris quite short like the French do. It is therefore not surprising that, in France, we should say Confucius, instead of Koang-fu-tsee; first of all, because the Latin termination in *us* is much in honour in philosophic language, but also because one of our principles is—not to bother ourselves whenever there is anything difficult to pronounce. Hence the precaution, so much admired, of an artist of German origin; who, fearing to find his native cognomen replaced by one not to his liking, prepared his visiting card as under:

—SCHNEITZOEFFER.—

(Please pronounce BERTRAM.)

Well, Koang-fu-tsee or Confucius (or Bertram) was a great philosopher, as everybody knows; but, besides that, he had a great fund of musical science; so much so that, having composed some variations on the celebrated air, "Li-po," he executed them upon a guitar which was ornamented with ivory; and, proceeding in this way from one end of the Celestial Empire to the other, he improved the morals of the entire population. And that is how it is that, since that time, the Chinese people have been so profoundly moral.

But the work of Koang-fu-tsee is not confined to these famous variations for the guitar, ornamented with ivory. No; the great philosopher-musician wrote, besides that, a goodly number of moral cantatas; and moral operas the principal merit of which, according to all the literary and musical people of China, is a simplicity and a beauty of melodic style, united to the profoundest expression of the passions and sentiments. A remarkable fact is quoted of a Chinese woman, who, being present at an opera in which Koang-fu-tsee has painted with touching truth the joys of maternal love, as early as the seventh act, began to cry bitterly. As those near her desired to know the cause of her grief : " Alas !" said she, " I have given birth to nine children, but have drowned them all; and now I am sorry not to have kept, at least, one. I should have loved it so much."

Chinese legislators have, therefore, and with great reason as I believe, pronounced severe punishments, not only against theatre-directors who give bad representations of the beautiful lyric works of Koang-fu-tsee, but also against concert-singers who dare to sing fragments from them unworthily. Every week a report is made by the musical police to the mandarin-director of arts; and, if a *prima donna* is found guilty of the crime of profanation which I have just indicated, they call her attention to the fact by cutting off her left ear. If she is again guilty of the same crime they again remind her of the circumstance by cutting off the right ear; after which, if she lapses again into the same fault, punishment begins; and they cut off her nose. This case is very rare; and Chinese legislation, moreover, shows itself herein somewhat severe, in exacting an irreproachable execution from a *prima donna* without ears. The penalties of certain nations have something comic about them which always astonishes us. I remember, at Moscow, having seen a great lady of the Russian aristocracy, sweeping a street, in broad daylight, at the moment of the thaw. " That is the custom," said a Russian to me. " They have condemned her to sweep the road for two hours; in order to punish her for being caught, *flagrante delicto*, stealing in a draper's shop."

At Taïti, that charming French province, the insular beauties convicted of having had smiles for too great a number of men, whether French or Taïtian, are condemned to make, with their own hands, a certain portion (more or less long, paved or otherwise) of the roadway. Thus, gallantry is arranged to turn to the advantage of the roads of communication. How many women there are in Paris who never arrive at anything; and who, in that country, would certainly " make their way."

The title *director-of-arts*, which I employed just now for a mandarin, must have appeared strange. It is difficult to conceive the utility of such an art-direction amongst ourselves; where art is not only free to stray, but may, if it chooses, become beggar, thief, assassin or page to some great lord. It is free to die of hunger; or to wander, besotted, about the streets of our cities. Our singers, it is true, keep possession of their ears and noses; for the first condition required in order to become administrator of a theatre is not to know anything of music. With us it is the literary folk who are the arbiters in musical matters; and we appoint painters to award the prizes for musical composition. But prizes for painting are, in their turn, awarded by architects; and those for statuary, by engravers. How the Chinese would laugh, if they only knew! Poor Chinese!

However, I told you that there was some good in them. They have directors-of-arts who really understand what they direct; they have even entire colleges of mandarin-artists, the influence of which is capable of becoming immense; and of spreading, to the great advantage of art, over the entire empire. In China, no book is published upon music, painting, architecture, etc., without the author first submitting his production to the examination of the mandarin artists; in order, should they approve it, to be able to inscribe upon the second edition of the work:

"Approved by the College."

F

Unfortunately, the respected members of this institution, who would often have the right to visit authors with the punishment of the cangue, have always been, unlike the special directors for musical art, actuated by such benevolence as generally to approve whatever might happen to be submitted to them. On one day, they will praise an author for having exposed such and such a doctrine; extolled such and such a tamtam method. The next day, another author will demonstrate the opposite faith, and preach a system in total opposition to the former; but the college will not fail to approve him also. They have, in fact, arrived at such a degree of indulgence, that now, the generality of authors take their approval for granted; by placing, upon the first edition of their works, the formula:

"*Approved by the College*,"

before having submitted them for examination; so sure have they become of obtaining the requisite consent. Ah! these poor Chinese! There is no need to wonder that art with them should obstinately remain stationary; but, I pardon them everything, in consequence of that rule of theirs—about tamtams and against profaners.

But, now you will ask: "If they cut off the noses and ears of singers who profane works of art, what do they do for those who interpret them with fidelity, grandeur and inspiration?"

What do they do?—why they heap upon them honourable distinctions of all kinds. They give them
silver chop-sticks to eat their rice with. To some, they
give the yellow button; to others the blue button; and
to others the crystal button. The same artist may possess all three buttons; and, in China, some virtuosi are
to be seen *covered with buttons*. It is not like that in
France, where they only give the cross to a singer after
he has left the theatre; when he has lost his voice, and
is no longer good for anything.

Chinese manners may be different from ours in all
that concerns the fine arts in general, and music in
particular but they nevertheless resemble them on one
point; as the Chinese take sailors to direct their fleets.
If things continue in the same way, we shall assuredly
finish by resembling them altogether.

IX

ADDRESS TO THE MEMBERS OF THE ACADEMY OF FINE ARTS OF THE INSTITUTE

September 11, 1861

GENTLEMEN and Dear Colleagues,
    You are of opinion that an account of my doings at Baden at the present time would be likely to interest the audience at a public sitting of the Institute. I do not share your view*; but, as such is your desire, I acquiesce and write to you.

Do not, however, imagine that I deceive myself so far as to paraphrase the descriptions of Baden given with such rare talent by Eugène Guinot, Achard and some other authors. No; I shall speak of music, of geology, of zoology, of ruins of splendid palaces, of

---

* As a matter of fact, the letter appeared to be in a style too far removed from academic habits, and was not read at any public sitting. (Note to the French edition.)

philosophy and of morality. We shall evoke antiquity and the Middle Ages, in addit.on to examining the present time. I shall quote from the Apocalypse, from Homer, from Shakespeare, perhaps even from Paul de Kock. I shall criticise right and left, as usual, even disapproving some of your approbations; but you will be obliged to listen to me, as you have yourselves desired it.

"What things to put into a minuet!" said the great Vestris. "What things to put into a letter!" you may say. Calm yourselves; my letter will be quite ordinary, clear and concise, like a friendly communication; subject to my health, which is unsatisfactory, and to the whims of my neuralgia. I purposely allow this word to slip; in order that you may be able to say; when I become too tiresome: "That is his neuralgia!"

As a matter of fact, many people are deprived of wit and good sense, even when they are well; but it is the contrary with me, my mental defect being never so evident as when I am ill. I belong to this second category; happy enough to think that I do not belong to the third—to the class of people who have no common-sense in any case.

What is my occupation in Baden? My occupation is music; the very thing which is absolutely forbidden to me at Paris, for want of a proper hall; for want of money to pay for rehearsals; for want of time to carry them out properly; for want of public support—for want of everything.

M. Benazet, who, for five months, is the real king
of Baden, and who exercises his sovereignty to the
greater glory of art and the greater happiness of artists, about eight years ago treated me to something
like the following discourse :

"My dear sir, I give many concerts in the little
rooms of the Konversationshaus. All the pianists of
the world come successively; and there are, sometimes,
several of them there at one time. We have the greatest artists and the most eccentric virtuosi. We have
violinists playing the flute, and flautists playing the
violin. We have basses singing soprano; sopranos
singing bass; and, sometimes, singers who have no
voice at all. They are therefore, on the whole, very
fine concerts. However, although they pretend that
the ideal looks down upon the excellent, it is the ideal
I have in view. Will you come to Baden and organ-
ise, annually, a grand musical festival? I will place
at your disposition whatever you ask for in the way
of singers and instrumentalists, in order to render the
whole effect suitable to the dimensions of the great
hall of the Konversationshaus; and, especially, to the
style of the works which you perform. You shall
make your own programmes and fix your own rehearsal days. If you require the help of special artists, engage them; promising them, on my part, the
terms they require. I have every confidence in you,
and shall not mix myself up with anything; except
paying !"

"Oh Richard! O my King!" cried I, distracted at hearing these sublime words. "What! Is there a sovereign capable of adopting such a course? You leave everything to me; you actually choose a musician to direct a musical institution—a musical enterprise—a musical festival! You forsake the ways of all Europe! You actually do not take a ship-captain to direct your concerts; nor a cavalry-colonel; nor a lawyer; nor a goldsmith? It must be true, then, God has said: Let there be light!—and there—*is* light. But all this is in reversal of the most sacred customs. You are ultra-romantic and will cause them to cry—'Haro.' They will break your windows! You will be horribly compromised, and the other sovereigns will surely withdraw their ambassadors."

"Never mind," replied M. Benazet, "whatever may happen to the European concert, I am resolved. It is understood; and I rely upon you."

Ever since that time, every year, as the month of August approaches, a certain restlessness which I feel in the right arm suggests to me that I am shortly to have an orchestra to conduct. Thereupon, I am occupied with the programme; unless (as nearly always happens), its arrangement dates from the preceding season. All that then remains is—to come to terms with the gods and goddesses of song engaged for the festival, and to decide upon the selection of their pieces. For my own part I abstain from designating what should be sung; being too well aware of the respect due to these divinities from simple mortals. At the end of six weeks, we generally find that we can come to no understanding; the lady singers, especially, having the habit of changing their minds about ten times before the day of the concert.

At the present moment, for the festival which is due to take place in a few days, I do not yet know what duet the tenor and *prima-donna* are going to sing; though I have begged them to give me the name of it for the last three months. The tenor solo, however, was settled at once; though the modesty of one of our colleagues forbids me to say more than that it is admirable.

I take this occasion, gentlemen, to address to you a question. I am informed that you have lately approved a work on the art of singing, the author of which, unfortunately a man of intellect and talent, declares that it is not only the right, but the duty of the singer to embroider airs of expression; to change certain passages in them according to his own views; to modify them in a hundred different ways; in short, to pose as the collaborator of the composer, and to make up for his deficiencies. What do you consider the composer of such a beautiful air should do?— tell me frankly, in the case of a tenor putting this incredible theory into practice, and singing such a work, in the author's presence, in a manner to disfigure phrases which already have a true expression, a profound sentiment and a natural melodic style? How do you consider that his inner senses should be affected and aroused if this *traditore* took it into his head to make ever so slight additions to a passage which already breathes candour and innocence, ingenuous grace or a naïve terror of death? The composer does not favour suicide, I know; but if he had a pistol in his hand it might be dangerous for the tenor.*

Be assured, however, that nothing of that kind will happen at Baden; my tenor being a serious artist, who has never dreamed of such monstrosities. Moreover, I shall be there; and in the event of his being so deserted by his guardian angel as to be guilty of such *lèse-majesté* of art and genius at the general rehearsal, I should at once speak to the orchestra in the same way as I was compelled to do upon a similar occasion in London.

"Gentlemen," said I, "when we arrive at that passage, look well at me; and, should the singer dare to disfigure it as he has just now done, I will make the sign to you to stop short. I forbid you to play, and he will sing without accompaniment."

* * *

Can it be that you approve such insults and the theory by which they are supported? You?—Were you to die, and afterwards return with such an assurance from beyond the tomb, I should not believe it.

---

* This passage is slightly softened from the original which runs: "S'il avait un pistolet à la main, à coup sûr il lui brûlerait la cervelle." (Translator's note.)

But stay; I have here a pretty anecdote, which applies to this subject in every way. It is true; in support of which I may appeal to the testimony of another of our colleagues, who figures in it as the victim of à virtuoso. The *traditore* in this case is an instrumentalist. For we poor composers have to submit to be ill-treated by everybody;

by singers without talent—by bad players.

by bad orchestras————by voiceless choristers

by incapable conductors) by stage managers
  (whether lymphatic { by machinists
    or bilious)

by copyists————————by engravers

by string merchants———— by instrument-makers.

by architects who construct the halls

and finally by the "claqueurs," who applaud; and who applaud to such an extent that never, during the whole time that Mozart's "Don Giovanni" has been performed in France, has it been ever possible to hear the beautiful instrumental phrase which concludes the mask-trio; for the applause always drowns it.

In Germany, where there are no claqueurs by profession, the applause is better advised. It is not the custom there to applaud indiscriminately; and they begin by listening. I remember, once at Frankfort, being at a representation of "Fidelio," during which the public did not give a single sign of approbation. As I had freshly arrived, with my Parisian habits and ideas, I felt indignant. But, after the last chord of the last act, the entire house rose and saluted Beethoven's work with a thundering salvo of applause. This was all right; but it was really time.

Now, what was I about to tell you? O that neuralgia! Ah, I remember. It was about an anecdote of those brigand virtuosi who strangle great composers. The one I am speaking of did worse; for he strangled a member of the Institute. I see you shudder; but these are the facts.

Five years ago, they were giving at Baden a new and charming opera, composed expressly for the season, and entitled "Le Sylphe." They had engaged a harpist from Paris, to play the orchestral accompaniment for an important vocal number. Inwardly persuaded that a man of his value owed it to himself to make some commotion in Germany, since he had condescended to come; and persuaded also that the author of the opera would not write a solo for the harp which the action of the lyric drama in question did not naturally suggest, our harpist provided one for himself, by clandestinely writing what may be called a little harp-concerto. On the evening of the first representation of "Le Sylphe," just at the moment when, after the ritornello of the orchestra, the singer was about to commence the air, our virtuoso, taking advantage of a moment's silence, coolly began his "concerto," to the dismay of the conductor, of all the band, of the singer, and of the unfortunate composer; who, perspiring with anxiety and indignation, thought he was in the middle of some horrid dream. I was there. The composer is philosophical, and accordingly did not lose much of his *embonpoint* over the affair; it was I who got thin for him. Now, gentlemen, do you approve of the harp-concerto?—and of this compulsory collaboration of virtuoso and composer?

I should also say that this same harpist, a few days before, had played in the orchestra of the festival; being seated near me. Noticing that he left off playing in a tutti, I said—"Why do you not play?"—"It would be useless," said he, "they would not hear me." He did not admit that it was either useful to the ensemble, or suitable for himself, to play without his harp being remarked amongst all the other instruments; so that, if this doctrine were in force, we should, at every instant, nearly always in the tuttis, have the second-flute, the second-oboe, the second-clarinet, the third and fourth horns, and all the violas giving the same reason for leaving off playing. There is no need to tell you that this noble aspirant has not again set foot, and never will set foot, in any orchestra placed under my direction.

Such suppressions happen rather rarely; but the system of additions, on the contrary, is in full force. The consequent disaster may be rendered more striking by supposing these practices applied to literature.

There are people who recite in public fragments of poetry, by placing them more or less in relief by their style of elocution. For the most part they seek applause by forcing the diction; exaggerating the accents, emphasising the words, or pompously pronouncing simple expressions, etc. If one of these, in reciting the fable of La Fontaine:

"La Mort et le Mourant,"

were to form the idea of introducing words of his own, in order to obtain greater effect, it is likely enough (as we must, unfortunately, admit) that there are minds so constituted as to absolve him from this insolence; and to regard even as ingenious the addition of spurious lines to those of the immortal fabulist. Let us suppose him proceeding thus:

> La mort ne surprend point le sage
> Il est toujours prêt à partir
> Sans gémir.*

"Without a sigh," he will remark, "why sigh?—when he is sure that all complaint will be in vain, and that nothing can delay the fatal moment? La Fontaine did not think of that. Therefore:

> Il est toujours prêt à partir
> Sans gémir
> S'étant su lui-même avertir
> Du temps où l'on se doit résoudre à ce passage
> D'usage.†

---

* The wise man's e'er prepared to bid
Adieu to life, when Death is nigh,
Without a sigh.

† Adieu to life, when Death is nigh,
Without a sigh;
For e'er the day he has to die,
A warning bids him meet the lot which doth befall
Us all.

"Ah! that is admirable," our Philistines will say, "certainly, nothing is more applicable to *us all* than death; and this short line, placed in this way after an alexandrine, is of an intention so excellent that La Fontaine would have been sure to approve it, if it had been written in his time."

Confess now; confess that, were you witnesses of such a literary abomination, far from acting like those complacent judges who are always ready to support the insulters against the insulted, you would demand for this reciter of La Fontaine

Un cabanon
A Charenton.*

The above, and worse still, would only represent what goes on in music every day.

It would not appear, however, that all composers show themselves openly indignant at being corrected by their interpreters. Rossini, for instance, seemed quite pleased to hear of the changes, embroideries, and of the thousand villainies which singers introduced into his airs.

"My music is not yet finished," said this terrible banterer, one day; "they are still working at it." "It will only be when nothing of mine is left that it will have acquired its full value."

At the last rehearsal of a new opera:

---

* A cell at Charenton.

"This passage does not suit me," said a singer, naïvely, "I shall have to change it."

"Yes!" replied the composer, "put something else in its place; sing the 'Marseillaise.'"

These ironies, however harsh they may be, will not remedy the evil. Composers are wrong to joke upon this subject, as singers thus find occasion to say—"He laughs, he is disarmed." He must be *armed*, on the contrary, and *not laugh*.

Another example, reverse in sense, but still analogous.

A celebrated conductor, who was reputed to have deep veneration for Beethoven, used nevertheless to take deplorable liberties with that master's works. One day, he happened to come into the café where I was; and in an evident state of great excitement.

"Ah! deuce take it!" said he, as soon as he perceived me. "You have just been the cause of my suffering a nice insult!"

"How so?"

"I have just come from the rehearsal of our first concert. When we began the scherzo of Beethoven's Symphony in C minor, the double-basses would insist upon playing; and, when I stopped them, they invoked your opinion, in blame of the suppression that I have made of the double-basses in that passage."

"What!" I replied. "Those wretched fellows have had the audacity to disapprove of you, and the still

greater audacity to play the double-bass part just as
Beethoven wrote it. That calls for vengeance."

"Bah! Bah! You are joking. The double-basses
do not produce a good effect there. I took them out
more than twenty years ago, because I like the violoncellos alone better. You know very well that, when
a new work is mounted, the conductor must always
arrange something."

"For my part, I have never heard of that. I only
know that, when a new work is studied for the first
time, the conductor and his musicians should, first of
all, try to understand it; and, afterwards, to perform
it with scrupulous fidelity united to inspiration, if
possible. That is all I know. If, after he had written the symphony, you had asked Beethoven to correct
it; and, if he had consented to touch it up from top
to bottom in order to please you, that would appear
quite natural. But you, without authorisation and
without authority, to apply your hand to a symphony
of Beethoven, and correct the orchestra in it, is one
of the most extravagant examples of temerity and
irreverence that could be sighted in the whole history
of art. As to the effect produced by the double-basses
in that place, and which you say is bad, that does not
concern you, or me, or anybody. The double-bass
part is written by the author, and must be executed;
moreover, your sentiment will certainly not be shared
by other conductors who follow your example. You
prefer that the theme of the scherzo should be taken

by the violoncellos; but another conductor will like the bassoons better, and another one the violas; so that the composer will be the only man who has no say in the matter. This is disorder at its climax; the collapse of art. If Beethoven revisited the world, and, hearing his symphony thus arranged were to ask who had *dared* to give him a lesson in instrumentation, you would cut a singular figure in his presence; as you must admit. Would you venture to answer— *I did it?* Lulli only broke a violin one day on the head of a musician, at the Opera, who failed in proper respect to him. It would not be a violin, but a double-bass, that Beethoven would break on your head; if he saw himself insulted and defied in such a way."

After a moment's reflection, striking with his fist upon the table, my man exclaimed:

"All the same the double-basses shall not play!"

"Oh! as to that, those who know you would not expect it; we shall wait."

He died. His successor thought proper to reinstate the double-basses in their functions in the scherzo. But this change was not the only one committed in this splendid symphony. In the finale there is a repeat, indicating that the first part of the movement should be played twice, but which had been suppressed on account of the repetition causing too great length. The new conductor had done justice to Beethoven as against his predecessor by reinstating the

G

double-basses, but he supported the old conductor against Beethoven by maintaining the suppression of the repeat (observe the exercise of free-will by these gentlemen; is it not admirable?)

The new conductor also died; and now, if Mons. T——, who replaces him, does complete justice to Beethoven, as seem probable, he will reinstate the repeat, and thus three generations of conductors, and thirty-five years of efforts on the part of Beethoven's admirers will have been necessary in order to get this marvellous work of the greatest of all instrumental composers performed at Paris, just as the author conceived it.

Certainly gentlemen you will not approve of that; and yet it is but the natural result of tolerating the insubordination of certain executants, and the insensate prerogative which they claim to correct the works of authors.

One of our most illustrious virtuosi has thus expressed himself upon this subject:

"We are not the mere staple by which the picture is suspended; we are the sun by which it is illumined."

To this, it may be replied:

In the first place, we admit this modest comparison. But the sun, in lighting up a picture, reveals its exact design and colour. It does not cause either trees or weeds to grow; or birds or serpents to appear, where the painter has not placed them. It does not change the expression of the figures; and render the gay faces sad, or the sad faces gay. It does not enlarge certain outlines, and reduce the extent of others. It does not make black white, and white black; in short it shows us the picture as the master painted it. We do not wish for anything other than that which you propose. Be therefore the suns; ladies and gentlemen, and we shall be happy to adore you. Be really suns; and try not to make of yourselves cellar-rats and rag-picker's lanterns.

* * *

I ascended to the old castle with great strides; and enraged with all my soul, at being obliged to recognise that great poets, like great artists, are fatally destined to be outraged in a thousand ways; that, if the "Iliad" were transformed into a vaudeville, or the "Odysee" into a ballet: if a pipe were placed into the mouth of the Farnese Hercules, or a moustache drawn upon the lip of the Venus of Milo; if the practitioners were to correct the work of statuaries, or to mutilate the masterpieces of musical art; there would be no one to avenge them, and our governors would not condescend to occupy themselves with the matter.

* * *

The old castle of Baden is a colossal ruin of the Middle Ages, a nest of vultures constructed at the summit of a mountain which dominates the entire Oos-Thal. In the middle of a forest of gigantic fir-trees we see, on all sides, the remains of walls, black and hard as rocks, and portions of rocks as upright as the walls. Oaks of centuries ago have taken possession of the courts; the leafy heads of curious old beeches pass by the windows; interminable staircases and bottomless wells present themselves at each instant before the steps of the astonished explorer, who can scarcely resist a feeling of secret terror. There, once lived, we know not when, nor do we know their names, landgraves, margraves or burgraves; human birds of prey, past-masters in brigandage, murder and rapine that civilisation has caused to disappear. What crimes have been committed under those formidable vaults! what cries of despair and what sounds of cruel orgies have those panels caused to resound! Nowadays, oh prosy age of flat utility! A restaurateur is in possession; and the only noises we hear come, either from the furnaces of a vast kitchen, from the explosion of bottles of champagne, or from the laugh of the German townsmen and French tourists, enjoying themselves. However, if we have the courage to undertake the ascent of the ruined summit of the monument, we gradually find solitude, silence and poetry. From the height of the last platform we can perceive, in the plain on the other side of the mountain, several happy little German towns; fields well cultivated; a luxuriant vegetation; and the Rhine, sad and silent, winding its interminable silver way to the horizon.

It is to that spot that I arrived, still complaining like an impatient locomotive. Gradually, calm and indifference came back to me, whilst listening to the mysterious voices which speak there with an equal indifference and calm; but always of men and times which are no more.

The love of music itself seemed to be revived in me while listening to the ineffable harmonies of the Æolian harps; placed, by some charitable German, in the intricacies of the ruins, where the winds cause them to give out such poetic plaints. These vaporous chords give an idea of the infinite; we cannot tell when they begin or end; and often think we hear them, after they have ceased vibrating. They awaken in us vague remembrances of youth departed; or expired love; and of hopes deceived. We sadly weep; but that is only if we are not too old, for then the eye refuses to respond; preferring to close and yield to drowsiness.

It seems that I am not yet to be classed with the old, since I did *not* yield to drowsiness. Far from that; for, after a shower, the sun reappeared, and I began to think of a little work which occupies me just at this moment. Seated on a battlement, I started writing the lines of a night-scene, for which, in the next few days, I shall try to find music. Here it is :

Nuit paisible et sereine !
La lune, douce reine
Qui plane en souriant,
L'insecte des prairies
Dans les herbes fleuries
En secret bruissant
    Philomèle
    Qui mêle
Au murmure du bois
Les splendeurs de sa voix ;
    L'hirondelle
    Fidèle
Caressant sous nos toits
Sa nichée en émois ;
Dans sa coupe de marbre
Ce jet d'eau retombant
    Écumant
L'ombre de ce grand arbre
En sceptre se mouvant
    Sous le vent ;
    Harmonies
    Infinies,
Que vous avez d'attraits
Et de charmes secrets
Pour les âmes attendries !*

I had proceeded thus far with my nocturne, when one of the geese, which are so numerous at Baden just now, appeared suddenly to call me back to prose: "Oh! it's you!" it seemed to say to me, in that well-known voice which once was saviour of the Capitol,

---

* O, serene and peaceful night, with the sweet pale moon passing gently overhead; with the insects of the fields rustling amidst the flowery grass; and Philomèle uniting the splendours of her voice with the murmur of the woods. Whilst the swallow under the roof-tree faithfully tends its little brood; the fountain-flow returns to its basin all foaming; and the shadows of the great trees wave like sceptres in the wind, with its infinite harmonies. What attractions have you not—what secret charms for loving souls!

"what the deuce are you doing there, all alone, perched on that dungeon? Ah! poetry? Let me look! I bet that you are working at the opera which M. Benazet has ordered you to write for the opening of the Baden theatre. It's getting on—is this new theatre; and will be finished next year. The builder of it is a little old, it is true, but still vigorous; and it is he who worked with so much ardour at Paris, before 1830, to build the 'Arc de Triomphe de l'Étoile.'"

"Precisely, my dear fellow, I am busy with that little opera; but please do not employ expressions so unsuitable. M. Benazet has not *ordered* me at all; and you ought to know that art is never 'ordered.' They *order* a French regiment to go and get itself killed; and it goes. Or, they *order* the crew of a French vessel to go and get blown up; and they go. They can also *order* a French critic to go and hear a comic opera which he has to write about; and he goes. But that is all; we cannot *order* certain actors to go so far as to disturb their habits and to be simple, natural, noble and equally removed from platitude and exaggeration! We cannot *order* certain singers to have some soul, or to rhythmise properly. Nor can we *order* certain critics to know what they are talking about, certain writers to respect grammar, or certain composers to know counterpoint; for artists are proud, and would not obey. For my part, anyone who *orders* me to do anything may be sure that the effect is to paralyse me and render me stupid; and, as I believe you to be organised in the same way, I beg you most earnestly ' it would be useless to *order* you' I conjure you to redescend to Baden, and to leave me here, on my dungeon, to dream."

That goose went off with a sneer. But the thread of my ideas was broken; and, after some useless efforts to renew it, I stayed unthinkingly listening to the Austrian Emperor's hymn, which was being played, far away in the Kiosk of the Konversations-haus, by the Prussian military band; and the strains of which were carried to me in fragments from the depths of the valley, by the south wind. How touch-ing is that melody of good old Haydn! What traces it contains of a certain religious warmth! It seems a real song of people who love their King. Pray do not think I use the term "good Haydn" in any mock-ing sense; no, God forbid! I have always felt in-dignant against Horace, that Parisian poet of ancient Rome, for daring to say:

Aliquando bonus dormitat Homerus.

Haydn is certainly not to be dubbed "good-man"; but, rather, a man who was good; and proof lies in the fact that he had an insupportable wife who was never beaten by him, though they do say that he some-times allowed himself to be beaten by her.

At last the night began to fall, and I was obliged to descend:

La lune, douce reine
Planait en souriant.*

I re-crossed the pine-forest, which is more sonorous and of better sonority than most of our concert-halls, and in which even quartets might be performed. I have often thought of a piece which would be admirable if performed there on a beautiful summer-night; and that is, the act of the Elysian Fields, in Gluck's "Orphée." I fancy I can hear, under that dome of verdure and in semi-obscurity, that chorus of happy shades, the melodious charm of which is increased by the Italian words:

Torna o bella ali tuo consorte,
Che non vuol che più diviso
Sia di te pietoso il ciel.

But, when one has these musical fancies in the wood it is always after an enjoyable mid-day meal, and that is the precise moment they choose to perform fanfares—hunting fanfares; which wake up no other ideas than those of dogs, huntsmen and wine.

In the midst of the whole scene there is a spring, running along with a slight murmur, and near the basin of which I went to repose myself. I should have remained there until the next day, listening to its tranquil song, if it had not so reminded me of the springs of the interior corridor of the Grande-Chartreuse, which I heard for the first time thirty-five

* The sweet pale moon was passing gently overhead.

years ago. (Alas! thirty-five years.) The Grande-
Chartreuse made me think of the Trappists, and of
their continual phrase :

Frère, il faut mourir !*

This lugubrious phrase recalled to me that I had to
go early the next day to Carlsruhe, for the rehearsal
of the choruses of my Requiem; as our programme
for this year contains two numbers from that work.
So, I returned to my lodging to prepare for the
journey.

"Where can be his senses," you will say, "to give
the people, who are at Baden for their pleasure, pieces
to listen to, taken from a mass for the dead."

That is precisely the antithesis which charmed me
in making the programme; for it seemed to me like
the realisation in music of Hamlet's idea, when he was
holding the skull of Yorrick: "Now get you to my
lady's chamber, and tell her, let her paint an inch
thick to this favour she must come; make her laugh
at that."

"Yes, make them laugh"; I said to myself, also;
"all those crinolined beauties, so proud of their young
charms; of their old name; and of their numerous
millions; make them laugh, those bold women who
spread contamination and ruin; make them laugh,
those dealers in bodies and souls, those abusers of

---

* Brother! we must die!

the sufferings of poverty"; by singing to them the
redoubtable poem of an unknown poet, whose bar-
barous rhymed Latin of the Middle Ages invests his
threats with a peculiarly frightful accent :

> Dies iræ, dies illæ
> Solvet sæclum in favilla :
> Teste David cum Sibylla.
>
> Quantus tremor est futurus
> Quanto judex est venturus
> Cuncta stricte discussurus !
>
> Tuba mirum spargens sonum
> Per sepulcra regionum,
> Coget omnes ante thronum.
>
> Mors stupebit et natura
> Cum resurget creatura
> Ludicanti responsura.
>
> Liber scriptus proferetur
> In quo totum continetur
> Unde mundus judicetur.
>
> Judex ergo cum sedebit.
> Quidquid latet apparebit :
> Nil inultum remanebit.

Make them laugh at those ideas; and, as the great
majority of the audience know nothing of Latin, I
must take particular care that the French translation
is printed with the programme, to "make them laugh."

What a poem—what a text for a musician ! I
should be quite unable to express the agitation of my

heart, when, directing an immense orchestra, I arrive at the line:

Judex ergo cum sedebit.

Then all is black around me; I see no more, and fancy myself falling into eternal night.

"You seem to think your audience all destined to eternal punishment," you will say; and I must admit that my apocalyptic tirade might suggest that notion, though it is merely the current of Shakespearean ideas which has borne me along. It is, in fact, quite the contrary; for the fine society of Baden consists of honest folk who need to have no fear in dwelling upon the thought of a future life. The number of scoundrels among them is very small—and consists just of those who do not come to the concerts.

You may also ask me how, in such a small town, I should be able to get together the full equipment required for performance of this "Dies Iræ"; an equipment the elements of which are so difficult to secure in Paris. There is also the question of how to place them in the festival-hall; as well as that of how to bear with such a tremendous sonority. Firstly, you must understand that I have arranged the kettle-drum score for three players only. As to the brass,

Mirum spargentes sonum,

we easily obtained what we required by uniting the artists of Carlsruhe to those of Baden; and adding to them Prussian musicians from the garrison of Rastatt, a fortress near Carlsruhe. The chorus, which has been collected by the care of M. Strauss, maître de chapelle, and M. Krug, chorus-director to the Grand Duke, has now been a fortnight rehearsing; whilst instrumental rehearsals take place every three weeks, and everything proceeds with perfect regularity. Two days before the concert, I shall take our artists by rail to Carlsruhe; there to rehearse, with those of the grand-ducal chapel. But, on the day of the concert, early in the morning, M. Strauss will bring the artists from Carlsruhe to rehearse with those of Baden, on a vast platform, which will have been erected during the night, at one end of the hall of the Konversations-Haus. Play is suspended for that day. Behind the orchestra there will be a tribune of fairly good size; upon which I shall place my kettle-drum arrangement, together with the brass instruments. M. Kennemann, the intelligent and devoted bandmaster of Baden, will conduct them. These formidable voices and tones of thunder will, I trust, not lose anything of their musical power through being sent from such a distance. Moreover, the movement of the *tuba mirum* is so broad that the two conductors, by taking pains with both eye and ear, will be able to keep together without accident.

You see that I shall have a heavy day. From nine in the morning till noon, last general rehearsal; at three, re-arrangement of all music in the orchestra, which will have been more or less disturbed at the morning rehearsal; this is a duty which I dare not entrust to anyone. Then, at eight in the evening, the concert.

At midnight, under these circumstances, I am not quite in the mood to dance. But the Princess of Prussia (now Queen) generally attends this festival, and often deigns to engage me for a few moments for her observations upon the principal items of the programme; and these are always kind, notwithstanding her keen criticism. She speaks with so much charm; she so intimately understands music; she has so much sensibility, united to a rare intelligence; and she possesses so well the art of encouraging you, and giving you confidence, that, after five minutes of the charming interview, all my fatigue seems to have disappeared, and I should be ready to begin again.

The above, gentlemen, is what I am doing at Baden. There are other details which I might have given you; but God preserve me from continuing; for I can see, even from here, that half your audience are . . . . asleep.

X

THE PITCH

THE Minister of State, uneasy respecting the future, more and more alarming, of musical execution in lyric theatres; astonished at the shortness of duration of the singer's career; and rightly persuaded that the progressive elevation of pitch is a cause of the ruin of the best voices; has just appointed a commission, carefully to examine into this question, ascertain the extent of the evil and discover a remedy for it.

Whilst waiting for this gathering of specialists, consisting of composers, physicians and musical scholars, to resume its labours which have been suspended during the month now expiring, we propose to endeavour to throw some light upon the whole collection of facts; and, without any prejudice to the views which the commission may adopt, to submit to it, beforehand, our observations and our ideas.

HAS THE PITCH REALLY RISEN,* AND, IF SO, HOW MUCH DURING THE LAST HUNDRED YEARS?

Yes, unquestionably; the fact of its rise being recognised by all musicians and singers, as well as throughout the entire musical world, the progression followed by the rise seeming to have been approximately the same everywhere. The difference now existing between various orchestras in the same town, or between the orchestras of countries separated by considerable distances, generally consists of nuances not sufficient to prevent the occasional union of these orchestras; and, by means of certain precautions, to form of them one grand instrumental mass, the agreement of which, in respect of pitch, is satisfactory. If there were, as we are very often assured in Paris, a great difference between the pitch of the Opera, the Opera-Comique, the Théâtre-Italien and the military bands, how would it have been possible to form the orchestras of seven to eight hundred musicians which I have often had to direct in the vast spaces of the Champs Elysées, after the exhibitions of 1844 and 1855, as well as in the church of St. Eustache; considering that the elements of this musical congress necessarily

---

* I here employ the terms generally adopted of *high* and *low*, as also the verbs *ascend* and *descend*, which have no real application and which nothing but an absurd custom has sanctioned in our musical terminology in order to distinguish between the resultant sounds of rapid and slow vibrations.

consisted of nearly all the instrumentalists disseminated throughout the numerous musical bodies of Paris.

The festivals of Germany and England, for which the orchestras of several towns are frequently combined, prove that the differences of pitch are, there also, but slightly felt; and that the precaution of *drawing the slide*, in the case of wind-instruments which happen to be too sharp, suffices to obviate them.

Yet, however small they may be, these differences exist. The proof of this will shortly be in hand, as the commission has written to all the bandmasters, concert-directors and conductors in those towns of Europe and America where musical art is mostly cultivated, to ask them for a sample of the steel instrument which, under various names, they employ, as we do, to give the note A to the orchestra; and in the tuning of organs and pianos. These contemporary intonations, compared with those of 1790, 1806, etc., of which we are in possession, render the difference which exists between our present-day pitch and that of the close of the last century both evident and precise. Besides that, the old organs in various churches, on account of the special nature of the functions to which divine-service has restricted them, never having been placed in relation with the wind-instruments of theatres, have preserved the pitch of the period at which they were constructed; and this pitch is, in general, a tone lower than that which is now in use.

Hence arises the custom of giving these instruments

H

the name of organs in "B flat"; because their C, being
a tone lower than ours, is in unison with our *B flat*.
These organs are at least a century old; and we are
therefore bound to conclude from all the facts, which,
however different, agree amongst themselves, that, as
the pitch has risen a tone in a hundred years, or a
semitone in fifty years, if the same ascent continues,
it will, in six hundred years, traverse the whole twelve
semitones of the scale, and thus necessarily amount,
by the year 2458, to the rise of a complete octave.

The absurdity of such a result is sufficient to show
the importance of the step taken by the Minister of
State; and it is highly regrettable that one or other
of his predecessors has not thought of adopting similar measures long ago.

But, until now, music has rarely obtained any en-
lightened or official protection; notwithstanding that,
of all the arts, it is the one which stands most greatly
in need of it. At nearly all times, and in nearly all
places, its fate has been committed to the hands of
agents who had neither the sentiment of its power,
grandeur or nobleness, or the possession of any acquaintance with its nature, or means of action.
Always, and everywhere until now, it has been treated
like a Bohemian; expected to sing and dance in the
public squares, in the company of monkeys and performing dogs, and covered with tinsel to attract attention from the crowd, for the mere purpose of col-
lecting money.

The decision taken by the Minister of State gives occasion to hope that music in France will shortly have the protection it requires, and that other important reforms in the practice and the teaching of the art will follow closely upon the reform of pitch.

BAD EFFECTS OF THE RISE IN PITCH.

At the time when they commenced to write dramatic music in France, and to produce operas, as, for example, at the time of Lulli, the pitch, being established though not fixed (as we shall shortly see), the singers, whoever they might be, experienced no trouble in singing the parts written within the limits then adopted for voices. When, later on, the pitch had become appreciably higher, it was both the duty and interest of composers to recognise the fact by writing slightly lower; but they did not do so. Notwithstanding that, the parts written for Paris theatres by Rameau, Monsigny, Grétry, Gluck, Piccini and Sacchini, at a time when the pitch was about a tone lower than it is now, remained for a long time singable. The greater part of them are so still; which shows what an amount of prudence and reserve these masters exhibited in the use of voices. Exception must be made, however, of certain passages, occurring especially in Monsigny; the melodic tissue of which is disposed in a region of the voice already high for his period, and much too much so for ours.

Spontini, in the "Vestale," in "Cortez" and "Olympie," even wrote tenor-parts which our present-day singers find too low.

Twenty-five years later, during which the pitch had rapidly risen, high notes for tenors and sopranos became more frequent. There appeared also the high C natural, both in head and chest voice in tenor-parts; as well as the high C sharp, for the same parts, in head voice, it is true, but even that no ancient composer ever thought of employing. The necessity for the high B natural, given with force in chest-voice, became more and more frequent; and it must be remembered that this, in the old pitch, would have amounted to C sharp; of which there is not the slightest trace in the scores of the last century. To this, must be added the high C; attacked and sustained by sopranos, as well as the high E natural; which became usual in bass-parts. This last note was too often employed by the old masters, under the name of F sharp, at the period of the low pitch. Still, it was not used with anything like the same frequency as the E natural, which is its present-day equivalent.

On the whole, these excessively high intonations became so frequent, that the singer could no longer *emit* them, but was obliged to *extract* them, with violence; after the manner of a vigorous operator extracting a decayed tooth. After full consideration, the evidence allows us no alternative but to adopt the strange conclusion that grand opera in France was written for, higher and higher, whilst the pitch was also gradually rising. One can easily become convinced of this by comparing the scores of the last century with those of the present day.

Achille, in "Iphigenia in Aulide," which is one of the highest tenor-parts of Gluck, rises only to B natural; which was, of course, only equivalent to our present A. In one single instance he wrote, in "Orphée," a high D; but this one note, which was only the same sound as the C employed in "Guillaume Tell," occurs in slow vocalisation for head-voice, so that it is rather "touched" than intoned; and presents neither danger nor fatigue for the singer. One of Gluck's great female parts, that of Alceste, contains the high B flat, emitted and sustained with force; but this, again, is only equivalent to our A flat. Who would hesitate now, when writing for a *prima donna*, to use A flat, A natural, B flat, B natural, and even C?

The highest female part written by Gluck is that of Daphné in "Cythère-assiégée." An air of this character:

Ah! quel bonheur d'aimer!

rises, with a quick run, as far as C (our B flat); and a general inspection of this part shows that it was composed for one of those exceptional singers, such as we find in every age, with what are called "light" voices; or, voices which are of extraordinary extent in the upper region, such as those of Mesdames Cabel,

Carvalho, Lagrange, Zerr and some others at the present time. Still, I repeat, Daphné's high C only
amounted to our B flat, which is quite a common note.
Madame Cabel and Mademoiselle Zerr give the high
F; Madame Carvalho attacks high E without fear;
and Madame Lagrange does not hesitate, even before
a high G of the flute.

The old composers, writing for the Paris theatres,
persisted only in pushing the low voices upwards;
why, I cannot tell. In their bass-parts there is very
little else than work suitable for baritones. They never
dared to take their bass-voices lower than B flat, and
even this note they very rarely used. It was looked
upon as proved at the Opera, as late as 1827, that
low sounds had no resonance, and could not be heard
in a large theatre. Bass-voices were therefore spoiled;
and the parts of Thoas, d'Oreste, Calchas, d'Agamem-
non and Sylvain, which I have heard sung by Dérivis,
the father, seemed to have been written by Gluck and
Grétry for baritones. Those parts, therefore, although
they were then singable by genuine basses, are no
longer so.

But neither Gluck nor his competitors would ever
have dared to ask their dramatic tenors or sopranos
for the high notes which I quoted just now; and
which are, at the present day, so abused.

These excesses of the most learned masters of the
modern school have certainly had deplorable results.
How many tenors have broken their voices on the high

chest-notes of B and C! How many sopranos have, instead of musical notes, given us cries of horror and distress, in the attempt to render passages belonging to the modern repertoire, which are too numerous even to be mentioned! Add to this that the intensity of dramatic situations often gives rise to an abnormal energy—not to say, brutality—of the orchestra; resulting in a sonority, so excessive in such cases, that singers are unconsciously tempted to redouble their efforts to make themselves heard, and thus to produce a description of howl, deprived of all human trait. Certain masters have, at least, had the forethought not to employ strong chords for the full orchestra, simultaneously with the most important vocal notes; and thus, by adopting a species of dialogue, have allowed the vocal part to remain uncovered. But many, on the other hand, have literally crushed it beneath an accumulation of brass and percussion instruments and these have, notwithstanding, acquired a name as models in the art of vocal accompaniment: what an accompaniment!

These faults, gross, palpable and evident in themselves, could not fail, when aggravated by the rise in pitch, to produce the sad results which now attract the attention of even the least attentive listeners at our theatrical performances; but the present high intonation has produced a further evil which will now be mentioned.

Horn, trumpet and cornet players can no longer

be sure of certain notes which were formerly in general use; the majority not being even able to attack them. Of these, we may cite the high G of the trumpet in D; the E of the trumpet in F (both of which notes give the effect of A); the high G of the horn in G; the high C of this same horn in G (a note employed by both Handel and Gluck, but which has now become impossible); and the high C of the cornet in A. At every moment, frayed and broken notes, vulgarly called *couacs*, appear to the detriment of an instrumental ensemble, sometimes composed even of the most excellent artists. Thus, we hear it said:

"Trumpet and horn players have no longer any *lip*? Why? Surely, human nature has not changed."

No; human nature has not changed, but the pitch has; and many modern composers seem to ignore the new conditions.

Causes which have Led to the Rise in Pitch.

It seems, now, to be an ascertained fact that the evil which we are now all called upon to deplore is one of which the guilt lies with the makers of wind-instruments. In order to give more brilliancy to their flutes, oboes and clarinets, certain manufacturers have clandestinely raised the pitch. The young virtuosi, into whose hands such instruments have first fallen, have been obliged, on entering an orchestra, to *draw the slide*; in order to place themselves in tune with the others. But, as this lengthening of the tube (and especially of that of the flute) disturbs its proportions, and consequently diminishes the truth of the intervals, such artists, little by little, abstained from having recourse to it. The whole mass of stringed-instrument players naturally followed (possibly even without knowing it) the impulse thus given by these sharp wind-instruments; for violins, violas and basses had only to give a slight further tension to their strings in order easily to adopt a raised intonation. After that, the other musicians, the elders of the orchestra, having charge of bassoon, horn, trumpet, second oboe parts, etc., tired with making useless endeavours to bring themselves up to the prevailing pitch, have quietly gone to the maker to get their tubes slightly shortened; to get them "cut" (for that is the term adopted) and so enable themselves to conform with the new pitch. The latter is thus fully installed, as far as the orchestra is concerned; but the same influence very soon reached to concerts, through the medium of pianos; the pitch of which was regulated by tuning-forks, by slightly shortening its branches, with the aid of a file.

This whole procedure, more or less avowed, but equally real in either case, was repeated, approximately, and everywhere, about every twenty years.

Nowadays, even organ builders follow the same movement, and tune their instruments to the high pitch. We certainly do not know the exact pitch for which Saints Gregory and Ambrose composed the plain-chant which they bequeathed to the ecclesiastical liturgy; but it is evident that, the more the pitch of church-organs is raised (providing of course that the organ is used in giving the pitch and that it does not transpose) the more the entire system of plain-chant is altered; and the more the vocal economy of sacred hymns becomes disarranged. The organ should either transpose, when it accompanies plain-chant (if tuned to modern pitch), or remain permanently fixed at the pitch of ancient instruments. The latter pitch should, however, be regulated with such reference to that now in use as to allow of orchestral instruments being added, by means of transposition. Thus, if the organ were three semitones below orchestral pitch, this would not prevent the combination of orchestra and organ; but would merely require that the former should play, for instance, in F, while the organ was playing in A flat.

Unfortunately, some organ-builders choose the very worst of medium courses, by constructing their instruments a quarter-tone below the usual pitch. I made a cruel experience of this a few years ago at the church of St. Eustache; where, for the execution of a "Te Deum," it was impossible, notwithstanding that all the sonorous tubes of the orchestra were lengthened, to bring the mass of instruments in tune with the new organ, which had been built scarcely three years before.

SHOULD THE PITCH BE LOWERED?

It is certain, in my opinion, that a lowering of the pitch could only be attended by benefit to the art of music generally, and to that of singing more especially; but it seems to me impracticable to extend such a reform to the whole of France. An abuse which is the result of a long succession of years is not to be destroyed in a few days; and musicians, both singers and others, who might appear to be the most interested in securing a lower pitch, would very likely be the first to oppose it. Firstly, it would collide with their present habits; and God only knows whether there exists in France a force more irresistible than that of habit. But, even supposing that an all-powerful will should intervene to cause the reform to be adopted, its realisation would cost enormous sums. Even without counting organs, it would be universally necessary to buy new wind-instruments for theatres and military bands, and to absolutely forbid the use of old types. And then, after the reform had been successfully effected, if the rest of the world did not follow our example, France would remain isolated with her low pitch; and excluded from the possibility of musical relations with other nations.

SHOULD WE ONLY FIX THE ACTUAL PITCH?

This is, I believe, the wisest course to take; and the means to effect it are already in our possession. Thanks to an ingenious instrument which the science of acoustics has acquired a few years ago, and which is called the syren, it is now possible to count, with mathematical precision, the number of vibrations given out per second by any sonorous body.

In adopting the A of the Paris Opera as the typical sound, or sonorous official standard, this A being presumably the result of 898 vibrations per second, all that we should have to do would be to place, in every concert or theatre orchestra, an organ pipe giving the exact sound designated. This pipe would alone be referred to for the A, and the present custom entirely discontinued of tuning to the oboe or flute, the former of which can easily cause the pitch to rise by increasing the pressure of his lips upon the reed, and the latter do the same by turning his embouchure a little outwards.

The wind-instruments would thus be in perfect tune with the organ-pipe. They should also remain, in the interval between the representations or concerts, kept in the same room where the organ-pipe is placed; which room should be, like a greenhouse, constantly maintained at the average temperature of the theatre when the audience is present. Thanks to this precaution the instruments would not be brought cold into the orchestra, and would not sharpen, in the course of an hour, in consequence of the breath of the executants, or of their being introduced to a warmer atmosphere. It follows that the wind-instruments of a theatre (of a theatre of the government at any rate) should never be taken away under any pretext, but remain in the allotted room as permanently as if they were its fixtures. Should any player remove his instrument—his flute or clarinet—for the purpose of getting it "cut," the misdemeanour would be at once discovered; as he would then be out of tune with the organ-pipe, which, as I have said, should be alone consulted. Finally, the official adoption by the government of the A of 898 vibrations would involve that every manufacturer circulating either wind-instruments, organs or pianos pitched differently, would be amenable to certain penalties, precisely in the same way as shopkeepers who sell by false measure or weight.

With such precautions once taken, and the regulations enforcing them well and rigorously maintained, it is quite certain that the pitch would not continue to rise.

But even this remedy would be useless for voices if composers continue to write the dangerous notes which I just now quoted; and, for that reason, authority should intervene to forbid at all events composers who write for subsidised theatres to employ the exceptional notes which have destroyed so many good voices. They might also be *advised* (censure being scarcely applicable to a score) to be more circumspect in the employment of violent means of instrumentation.

XI

THE TIME IS NEAR

MUSICAL art, just now, is making rapid progress in Paris. The time is near for its elevation to a great dignity. It will be made Mamamouchi.

Voler far un paladina
Ioc!
Dar turbanta con galera
Ioc! Ioc!
Hou la ba,
Ba la chou,
Ba la ba,
Ba la da!

Then, when it is too late, Madame Jourdain, as public reason, will appear, and exclaim: "Goodness me, this is madness."

Happily, it sometimes exhibits (outside the theatre) certain rays of intelligence, calculated to reassure its friends. Thus, we still have at Paris some concerts where real music takes place. We still have some virtuosi who understand and worthily execute the higher

class of works; besides listeners who receive them
with respect and adore them with sincerity.   It is just
as well to make a mental note of this in order to resist the temptation of jumping down a well, head
first.

*   *   *

On the second day after the representation, at the
Opera-Comique, of an indescribable work, by which
the public had been exasperated, we happened to find
ourselves in a musical drawing-room in company with
a few friends, when, after we had just been speaking
of the new and awe-inspiring production which we
had all heard a couple of days before, the question
was put:

"To what Messiah does this precious composer play
the part of John the Baptist."

We were naturally concerned about the fell disease
with which musical art appears for the moment to be
afflicted; of the strange doctors called to her aid; of
the undertakers who are already knocking at her door;
as well as picturing the masons who must surely be
engaged in sculping her epitaph, when some one conceived the happy idea of imploring Madame Massart
to play the grand F minor Sonata of Beethoven.   The
virtuosa graciously acceded to the request, and the
company soon entered into the terrible and sublime
charm of that incomparable work.   Listening to this
"Titan's music," executed with a convincing inspiration, with a fire well-controlled and skilfully regu-

lated, we soon forgot all the deficiencies, miseries, shames and horrors of contemporary music. We felt ourselves thrill and tremble with admiration in presence of the profound thought and impetuous passion which animate the work of Beethoven; a work still greater than his greatest symphonies; greater than anything else which he has written; and, therefore, superior to anything else which musical art has ever produced.

And, as the virtuosa remained at the piano exhausted after the last few bars of the finale, we gathered round and pressed her hands which had already become cold.

What could we say? We felt that we formed, in that little room, lost, as it were, in the middle of Paris, and into which no anti-harmony will ever be allowed to penetrate, a group to be compared with that in the picture of the Decameron exhibiting cavaliers and young beauties; a group evidently enjoying the embalmed air of a delightful villa whilst, everywhere around this oasis, the whole city of Florence was being devastated by the black pest.

XII

THE CONCERTS OF RICHARD WAGNER
THE MUSIC OF THE FUTURE

AFTER a vast amount of trouble, enormous expense, and numerous but insufficient rehearsals, Richard Wagner has succeeded in bringing forward some of his compositions at the Théâtre-Italien. Fragments taken from dramatic works lose, more or less, by being performed away from the surroundings for which they were destined. Overtures and instrumental introductions, however, gain by such removal; because when performed by a concert orchestra, they are rendered with more pomp and brilliancy than when played by an ordinary opera-orchestra, which is much less numerous, and less advantageously disposed.

The result of the experience ventured in connection with the Parisian public by the German composer was easy to be foreseen. A certain number of listeners, without either prepossession or prejudice, quickly recognised both the powerful qualities of the artist, and

I

the pernicious tendency of his system. A far greater number seemed unable to perceive in Wagner anything more than a violent will-power; and, in his music, nothing but a fastidious and irritating noise. The foyer of the Théâtre-Italien formed a curious sight, on the evening of the first concert, on account of the turmoil, the cries, and the discussions which seemed, at every moment, on the point of degenerating into blows. In such an event, the artist who has provoked such public emotion would like to see it go farther still; and would not be sorry to be present at a hand-to-hand fight between his partisans and his detractors; on the condition, of course, that his partisans gained the upper hand. Such a victory would have been improbable on this occasion; God being always on the side of the biggest battalions. The amount of nonsense, absurdity and even falsehood uttered on such occasions is truly prodigious; and proves incontestibly that, in France at any rate, when the question touches a kind of music other than that which runs the streets, passion and partisanship prompt every word; and neither good-sense nor taste has any chance of making itself heard.

Prepossessions, whether favourable or hostile, form the basis of most judgments, even upon the works of recognised and consecrated masters. A composer, once reputed to be a great melodist, is free, upon occasion, to write a work entirely deprived of melody; without risk of not being admired, for that same work,

by people who would have hissed it had it borne
another name. The great, sublime and entrancing
overture of "Leonora," by Beethoven, is classed by
many critics as an unmelodious work, although it is
full of cantabile and melodious effects in the allegro
as well as in the andante. The very same judges
who disparage it applaud, and often encore the overture of "Don Giovanni," by Mozart; in which there is
not a trace of what can properly be called melody,
but the latter is by Mozart, the great melodist!

They rightly admire, in this same opera of "Don
Giovanni," the sublime expression of the sentiments,
passions and characters. But, at the allegro of the
last air of Dona Anna, not one of these severe critics
who pose as appreciating musical expression, and are
so sensitive about dramatic suitability, is shocked at
the abominable vocalisation which Mozart has had
the misfortune to let fall from his pen; being incited
thereby by some demon whose name remains a mystery. The poor injured girl exclaims:

Peut-être un jour le ciel encore sentira quelque pitié pour moi.

and, thereupon, the composer has formed a series of
high notes in vocalisation, of staccato, cackling and
leaping character, which have not even the merit of
yielding the singer any applause. If there had ever
been, in any part of Europe, a public truly intelligent
and sensitive, this crime (for it is no less) would not

have remained unpunished; and the guilty allegro would have been removed from the score.

I should be able to quote a multitude of similar examples to prove that, with very rare exceptions, music is judged on the basis of prepossession only; and under the influence of a deplorable prejudice.

This will be my excuse for the liberty which I am about to take in speaking of Richard Wagner, according to my own personal feeling, and without taking any account of the various opinions expressed with regard to him.

He has ventured to compose the programme of his first concert exclusively of collective pieces; either choruses or symphonies. This was, to begin with, a defiance of the habits of our public, who love variety. Under this pretext, they often show themselves ready to manifest a noisy enthusiasm for a little song, well sung; for an empty cavatina, well vocalised; for a violin solo, well bowed upon the fourth string; or for variations, well tongued upon some wind-instrument; after having given a kindly, but cold, welcome to some great work of genius. They evidently think that the king and the shepherd are equal during their life-time.

There is nothing like doing boldly such things as are practicable at all. Wagner has just proved it; for his programme, although deprived of the sweets which allure children of every age at our musical festivals, was none the less listened to with a constant and very lively interest.

He began with the overture, "Der Fliegende Holländer," which is that of an opera, in two acts, which I saw performed at Dresden, under the direction of the composer in 1841; and in which Madame Schroeder-Devrient played the principal part. This piece produced upon me the same impression then which it has just now done. It starts off with an overpowering orchestral burst, in which we fancy we at once recognise the howlings of the tempest, the cries of the sailors, the wind whistling through the rigging, and the stormy noises of the sea in fury. This commencement is magnificent; and it imperiously seizes the listener, and carries him along. But, the same method of composition being afterwards constantly employed, one tremolo succeeding another, and one chromatic-scale only ceasing in order to be immediately continued by another effect of the same kind, without a single ray of sunlight coming to break through these dark clouds charged with electric fluid, and incessantly pouring down their merciless torrents without the slightest melodious design coming to the relief of their black harmonies, the attention of the listener begins to wane, is then discouraged, and finishes by giving way. This overture, the development of which appears to me excessive, already manifests the tendency of Wagner and of his school not to take account of the *sensation*; and to recognise nothing but the poetical or dramatic idea required to be expressed, without troubling whether the expression of that idea obliges the composer or not to transgress musical conditions.

The overture, "Der Fliegende Holländer," is vigorously instrumented; and the composer has secured, at the onset, an extraordinary effect with the chord of the naked fifth. Presented in this way this sonority takes an aspect which is both strange and thrilling.

The grand scene from "Tannhäuser" (march and chorus) is of superb brilliancy and pomp—qualities which are augmented by the special sonority of the key of B major. The rhythm, which is never troubled or complicated in its action by being combined with rhythmic dispositions of another kind, here assumes a knightly, august and virile aspect. Even without the aid of scenic representation, we feel that such music must accompany the movements of men who are valiant and strong; and are covered with brilliant armour. This piece contains an elegant melody, clearly designed; though not very original, as it recalls, by its form, if not by its accent, a celebrated theme from "Der Freyschütz."

The last return of the vocal phrase at the grand tutti is still more energetic than the preceding; thanks to the intervention of a bass-figure, consisting of eight notes in the bar, and contrasting with the upper-part which contains only two or three. There are, certainly, a few modulations which are rather hard and somewhat crowded together; but the orchestra imposes them upon the listener with such vigour and authority, that they are at once accepted without resistance. In short, this piece must be recognised as masterly; and instrumented, like all the rest, by a skilful hand. Both wind-instruments and voices are, throughout, sustained by a powerful propelling force; and the violins, written for with admirable ease in the upper part of their scale, produce the effect of dazzling sparks illumining the whole sonority.

The overture to "Tannhäuser" is, in Germany, the most popular of Wagner's orchestral pieces. Force and grandeur still reign supreme; but the effect of the method which the composer has chosen in this instance is, in my case at any rate, to produce an extreme fatigue. The overture commences by an andante maestoso—a sort of chorale of beautiful character, which, later on, towards the end of the allegro, reappears against a high accompaniment consisting of an ostinato violin passage. The theme of this allegro, composed of two bars only, is but slightly interesting in itself. The developments to which it afterwards gives rise bristle with chromatic successions, and with modulations and harmonies of extreme harshness; precisely as in the case of the overture to the "Fliegende Holländer." When, finally, the chorale reappears, its theme being slow and of considerable breadth, the violin passage which accompanies it right to the end is necessarily repeated so persistently as to be terrible to hear. It has already occurred twenty-four times in the andante; but, in the peroration of the allegro, we have it for one-hundred-and-eighteen times more. This "obstinate," or rather "desperate," design figures, therefore, altogether, no less than one hundred and forty-two times in the overture. Is this not too much? It reappears again very often in the course of the opera, however; so that I am tempted to suppose that the author attributes to it some expressive signification relative to the action of the drama, which I am unable to guess.

The fragments from "Lohengrin" are distinguished by more striking qualities than the preceding works. It seems to me that they contain more novelty than those from "Tannhäuser." The introduction, which takes the place of an overture for that opera, is an invention of Wagner producing a most remarkable effect. A visible idea of it is presented by the figure:

as it is, in reality, a slow and immense *crescendo*; which, after having attained its climax, follows the reverse progression and returns to the point from which it started, concluding with a harmonious murmur, scarcely perceptible. I do not know what relations exist between this form of overture and the dramatic idea of the opera; but, without concerning myself with this question, and considering it only as a symphonic piece, I find it admirable in every respect. There are no periods, properly so called, it is true; but the harmonic sequences which it contains are melodious and charming, whilst the interest never for a moment wanes, notwithstanding the extreme slowness of the *crescendo*, and that of the *diminuendo*. It is also a marvel of instrumentation, both in soft tints as well as in brilliant colours; and, towards the end, a remarkable feature is presented by the bass, which continues to rise diatonically whilst the other parts descend, and thus presents an idea which is most ingenious. This fine piece, moreover, does not contain the least harshness; being as suave and harmonious as it is grand, strong and sonorous. I regard it as a masterpiece.

The grand march in G, which opens the second act, has produced, in Paris as in Germany, a veritable commotion; notwithstanding the vagueness displayed at the commencement, and the cold indecision of the episodial passage in the middle. These insipid bars, in which the composer seems to be groping and feeling his way, are only a sort of preparation, in order to arrive at a formidable and irresistible idea, which is to be regarded as the real theme of the march. A phrase of four bars, twice repeated, with rise of a third, constitutes the vehement period with which perhaps nothing in music can be found to compare for noble rage and strength of demonstration. This phrase, launched forth by the brass in unison, converts the three strong accents, C, E, G (with which the three phrases begin) into so many tremendous cannon shots; which seem to shake the very breast of the listener.

I believe that the effect would have been more extraordinary still if the author had avoided such conflicts of sound as those which we have to suffer in the second phrase. In this, the fourth inversion of the chord of the major-ninth, and the delay of the fifth by the sixth, produce double-discords; which many people (including myself) cannot here tolerate. This march introduces the chorus in duple time:

Freulich geführt ziehet dahin

which we are startled to meet with in this place, the style of it being so small; not to say childish. Its effect upon the audience of the Salle Ventadour was rendered worse by the fact that the first few bars recall an insignificant piece from the "Deux Nuits" of Boïeldieu entitled:

La belle nuit, la belle fête!

introduced into the vaudevilles, and which everybody in Paris knows.

I have not yet spoken of the instrumental introduction to Wagner's last opera, "Tristan and Isolde." It is singular that the composer should have chosen to produce this at the same concert as the introduction to "Lohengrin," considering that, in both, he has followed the same plan. Here, again, we have a slow movement, begun *pianissimo*, increasing gradually to *fortissimo*, and returning to the nuance of its starting point, without any other theme than a sort of chromatic sigh; but full of dissonant chords, the harshness of which is still further increased by extensive modifications of the real notes of the harmony. I have read this again and again, besides listening to it with profound attention and an earnest wish to discover what it means, but am constrained to admit that I have still not the least idea of what the composer wanted to do.

The above sincere account brings out sufficiently the grand musical qualities of Wagner, and seems to me to carry the conclusion that he possesses the rare intensity of feeling the interior warmth and power of will, as well as the faith which subjugates, moves and convinces. But it also implies that these qualities would have worked more effectively had they been united to more invention, less research, and to a more just appreciation of certain constituent elements of art. So much for the practical part of the question.

Now, let us examine the theories which are said to be those of his school—a school which is now generally designated by the name of "music of the future" because it is supposed to be in direct opposition with the musical taste of the present time; and, also, certain to be found in perfect accord with that of a future period.

Both in Germany and elsewhere, opinions upon this subject have, for a long time, been attributed to me which I do not entertain. In the result, certain praise has been addressed to me which I could only interpret as blame; though I preserved a constant silence. But now, being in a position to explain myself categorically, no one I hope will consider that I ought still to keep silent, or halt in my profession of faith. Let us proceed, therefore, with entire frankness, and avow certain precepts to which it may be hoped that the school of the "music of the future" adheres.

*   *   *

1. "Music at the present day is in the force of its youth, is emancipated and free; is in a state of liberty to act."

2. "Many old rules have no longer any force; having been formulated by inattentive observers or by plodding minds for the use of plodders."

3. "Fresh needs have arisen; alike of the mind, heart and sense of hearing. These impose upon us new attempts; and even the occasional infraction of ancient precepts."

4. "Several forms have been too much employed to allow of their being considered as any longer admissible."

5. "*Everything is good;* or, *everything is bad;* entirely according to the use made of it, and the reason or motive by which such use is suggested."

6. "In its union with the drama, or even merely with words intoned by the voice, music should always be in direct relation with the sentiment verbally ex-

pressed; with the character represented by the singer; and, often, even with the accent and vocal inflections which are most natural to the spoken word."

7. "Operas should not be written for singers; but singers, on the contrary, trained for operas."

8. "Works written with the sole object of displaying the talent of virtuosi cannot aspire to be considered as compositions of more than secondary order, and of comparatively little value."

9. "Executants are merely instruments; more or less intelligent, destined to reveal the form and intimate sense of works. Their despotism is at an end. The master remains the master. It is for him to command."

10. "Sound and sonority are subservient to the idea. The idea is subservient to sentiment and passion."

11. "Long, rapid vocalisations; ornamentations; the vocal trill; and a multitude of rhythms are irreconcilable with the general expression of all serious, noble and profound sentiment. It is therefore insensate to write for a 'Kyrie Eleison' (that most humble prayer of the Catholic Church) passages liable to be mistaken for the vociferations of a group of topers round a tavern table. It is scarcely less insensate to employ the same music for an invocation to Baal by idolators, as for a prayer of the children of Israel addressed to Jehovah. It is most odious of all to take an ideal creation of the greatest poets, an angel of purity and

love, and give to it a form of exclamation expressive only of depravity." Etc.

*   *   *

If such is the musical code of the school of the future we belong to it, heart and soul, with profound conviction and the warmest sympathy.

But, then, everybody belongs to it. There is no one, nowadays, who does not more or less openly profess this doctrine; either entirely, or in part. Is there a master who does not write with full liberty? And who is there who believes in the infallibility of scholastic rules, unless it may be some timid old fellows who would be frightened at the shadow of their own noses?

But more still. It already has been so for a long time. In this sense, Gluck himself belonged to the "school of the future"; for he says, in his famous preface to "Alceste," that "there is no rule that he has not felt justified in sacrificing readily in favour of effect."*

And Beethoven, what was he, if not the boldest, most independent and the most impatient of all restraint amongst composers? Long even before Beethoven, Gluck had admitted the employment of "upper pedals," or long sustained notes in the upper part; although they do not enter into the harmony and pro-

---

* Il n'est aucune règle que je n'aie cru devoir sacrifier de bonne grâce en faveur de l'effet.

duce double and treble discords. He succeeded in drawing sublime effects from this act of boldness in the introduction of the infernal scene in "Orphée"; in a chorus of "Iphigenia in Aulide"; and, especially, in this passage of the immortal air of "Iphigenia in Tauride":

Mêlez vos cris plaintifs à mes gémissements.

M. Auber did the same, in the tarantella of "Masaniello." What liberties has Gluck not taken with the rhythm? In the "school of the future" Mendelssohn passes for a classic; but he, nevertheless, disregarded tonal unity in his beautiful overture of "Athalie"; which begins in F, and finishes in D; though this was no more than Gluck, who commences a chorus of "Iphigenia in Tauride" in E minor, and finishes it in A minor.

We are all of us, therefore, in one respect, of the "school of the future."

But, if this school proposes to us the following precepts; the case would be different.

* * *

1. "We must always, always go contrary to the rules."

2. "We are tired of melody, of melodic designs, of airs, duos, trios and of all pieces in which the theme is regularly developed; satiated with consonant harmonies; simple discords, prepared and resolved; and with modulations which are natural, and artistically regulated."

3. "We have no concern with anything but the idea; and, therefore, care nothing for the sensation."

4. "We despise the ear as a contemptible attribute, requiring to be tamed. The object of music has no reference to its pleasure. It must become accustomed to everything: to successions of diminished sevenths, ascending and descending, like troops of serpents, twisting and biting one another with a hissing sound; to triple discords, without preparation or resolution; to intermediate parts, obliged to go together without agreeing in respect of either harmony or rhythm, and which stand in one another's way; and to atrocious modulations, which introduce a tonality in one corner of the orchestra before the preceding tonality has departed from the other."

5. "We should hold the art of singing in no esteem; not trouble about its nature or its requirements; and, in an opera, we need only think of the declamation, to the neglect of whether the intervals employed are unsingable, absurd or ugly."

6. "No difference need be made between music destined to be read by a musician quietly seated at his desk; and that which has to be sung by heart, on the stage, by an artist obliged to give attention, at the same time, to his own dramatic action, and to that of the other actors."

7. "We have not to concern ourselves with possibilities of execution."

8. "If singers experience as much trouble in acquir-

ing a part and accustoming their voice to it as if they had to learn a page of Sanscrit by heart, or swallow a handful of nutshells, so much the worse for them. They are paid to work and are slaves."

9. "The witches in 'Macbeth' were right: 'Fair is foul, and foul is fair'; or, in other words, beauty is horrible, and ugliness beautiful."

*   *   *

If the above correctly represents the new religion, I am far from professing it. I never have accepted such principles, nor do I now, nor shall I ever do so. I raise my hand, and swear: *Non credo.*

My belief is, on the contrary, that beauty is not horrible and ugliness is not beautiful. No doubt the exclusive object of music is not to make itself agreeable to the ear; but, still less, should its object be to be disagreeable to it; to torture and assault it. Being simply human, I desire that my sensations should be taken into account and that such consideration should even be extended to my ear—that "guenille":

Guenille, si l'on vent; ma guenille m'est cher.*

I firmly reply, in this case therefore, as I one day replied to a great-hearted and intelligent lady who had been somewhat drawn aside by the same idea of liberty in art extended to the absurd. She said to me, in respect of a piece in which distorted means

---

* Rag, if you like; but a rag that is dear to me.

K

were employed, and about which I had refrained from expressing an opinion:

"But you must surely like that?"

"Oh! yes; I like that, just as I like drinking vitriol, or eating arsenic."

Later on, a celebrated singer who is now quoted as one of the most ardent antagonists of the "music of the future," paid me the same compliment. He had written an opera, in an important scene of which the Jewish rabble insults a captive. In order the better to render the hooting of the crowd, this realist wrote an eccentric chorus of continuous discords. Charmed by his own audacity, and opening his score at the place where the cacophony occurs, he said to me, with evident sincerity, I am pleased to say:

"I must show you that scene, you will surely like it."

I answered nothing; not even alluding to vitriol or arsenic. But considering that as I am now speaking this compliment comes back to me, I will take occasion to reply:

"No! my dear D——, that does *not* please me; but emphatically the contrary. It is a libel against me to assume that I can be in favour of such a charivari. They say that you are opposed to Wagner and his methods; but they have more right to class you among the rattle-snakes of the "music of the future"; you— a musician three-quarters Italian, and yet capable and culpable of this horror—than you have to place me, even among the eagles of that school; I—a musician

three-quarters German, who have never written anything of the kind, as I may easily contend, without
fear of contradiction.   Go and invite one of your own
way of thinking; order the cups of oxidised copper to
be brought in; pour out your vitriol; and drink.

As for me, I prefer water—even luke-warm; or even
an opera of

Cimarosa!

XIII

SUNT LACRYMÆ RERUM

IT is not sufficiently known, in general, how much labour is necessary to produce the score of a grand opera; or what a series of efforts, even more troublesome and painful, are required to ensure its presentation to the public. The composer, obliged to have recourse to two or three hundred intermediaries, is a man predestined to suffer; in spite of either moral influences or of real power disguised under any form.

Ni l'or ni la grandeur ne le rendent heureux,
Et ces divinités n'accordent à ses vœux
Que des biens peu certains, des plaisirs peu tranquilles.*

The only person who is out of reach of the thousand torments which the composition of a great musical work brings in its train is the great virtuoso whose gifts enable him to interpret his own inspirations. It

---

* Nor influence, nor gold, can render him serene,
To both the gods but vain recourse hath ever been,
Their joys ne'er brought him rest—their gifts the barrenest.

will be sufficient to say, that, for a certain style of
art, this kind of author is scarcely to be found; and
that, for dramatic, symphonic or religious music, which
necessarily requires the co-operation of a crowd of in-
telligences, animated by good-will, this paragon cannot possibly exist. Sophocles, they say, recited his
poems at the Olympic solemnities of Greece; and, by
that simple recitation, brought his immense audience
into a state of enthusiasm, even moving them to tears.
There, at least, is an example of the happy author;
powerful, radiant and almost divine! They listened
to him; they applauded him; and even divined his
meaning; to such a degree that four-fifths of his audience applauded, even without hearing.

Try, nowadays, to perform a work you have composed before even the tiniest audience of, say, six thousand persons; for what is that compared to the multi-
tudes which were attracted by the Olympic games?—
now, that composers sing even worse than singers by
profession; now, that they laugh at the lyre of four
strings, and want orchestras and choruses of eighty;
now, that insensate communism is such as to cause the
merest clown who has paid (or has possibly not even
paid) for his place in the pit to consider that he has
the *right* (a good old word, more clownish than long!)
to hear whatever is said, sung, cried or played, either
on the stage or in the most mysterious catacombs of
the orchestra; as well as everything howled or mewed
in the most hidden ranks of the chorus; now, that faith

in art no longer exists; at a time when, not only it cannot transport men, but when the very mountains remain deaf to its voice, and only answer its pressing appeals by an insolent inertia and irreverent immobility.

No; nowadays, we have to pay at once to obtain a success; and pay both dearly and often. Ask our great masters what their glory costs them, one year with another; they may not tell you, but they know. And, even when that glory is acquired; even when it has become an incontested and almost incontestible possession; do you think that it will serve them in the place of faith? Do you think that people nowadays are going to imitate the Athenians; and say, whilst they applaud:

"I cannot hear; but Sophocles is speaking, and what he says can be no other than sublime."

Quite the contrary. With every new work that our modern Sophocles produces his work begins again. Our modern Athenians, who can hardly be said to listen, but who nevertheless hear with all the length of their ears, take care, in such a case, not to applaud with the connoisseurs of the pit; and even laugh (the wretches!) at the ardour of that intelligent applause. It would be in vain to say to them: "It is Sophocles"; they either remain immovable as hills, or else play round success, like so many lambs.

It is just this playfulness which is most to be feared. Were I a Sophocles, I should prefer to see Mount Athos remain firm and cold before me, deaf to all my conjurations; rather than to be the centre of the joyous dances of a troop of Parisian lambs. Think what it would be if they were rams and goats!

All that remains, therefore, to compensate artists who produce their works with so much labour, and without thinking of their commercial value, is the inner satisfaction afforded by their conscience and the profound joy which they experience in measuring the amount of their progress on the road to the beautiful. One such artist advances hundreds of kilomètres; and falls at the very moment when he thinks he has obtained the prize. Another one advances still more; but without arriving, for the ideal is never attained. Another may advance less; but they all progress, however, and all prefer their progress, whatever it may be, with all its blazing sun and with all its thirst and fatigue to the fresh open shelter and invigorating drinks poured out by popularity for those aspirants who are unmindful of the inaccessible goal, and who turn their backs upon it.

*   *   *

We have now to add a rather sad observation upon the subject of the indifference of the fashionable public, not necessarily for art in general, but for the more serious enterprises of the theatre of the Opera. As at the first, so at the hundredth representation of a work; as at seven, so at eight o'clock; the occupants of the first seats are not to be seen. Even curiosity, that vulgar sentiment which is of such powerful influence upon most minds, seems powerless to move them at the present time. In fact, if the bill were to announce that, for the first act of a new opera, a trio would be sung by the angel Gabriel, Michael the archangel and St. Mary Magdalen, in person, that bill would be a failure; and the saint, as well as the two celestial spirits, would have to sing their trio before empty benches, and to an inattentive pit; just like ordinary mortals.

Another symptom, no less disquieting, is also now manifested. Formerly, during the entr'actes, the foyer of the theatre was pretty generally occupied in discussing the new work; which they always judged very severely, everybody declaring: "Detestable, wearying, no music"; and so forth. But, now, they say nothing; and it is no longer a question of the piece at all. They talk with eagerness about the Bourse; about the races at the Champ de Mars; of table-turning; or of the success of Tamberlick in London; of that of Mademoiselle Hayes at San Francisco; of the last hospital built by Jenny Lind; of the spring and of the state of the country. You hear: "I am starting for Baden"; "I am going to England"; or to Nice; or, it may be, only to Fontainebleau. And, if some primitive spectator, some man of the golden age, is rash enough, in the middle of such a conversation, to risk the absurd question:

"Well! what do you think of it?" they would answer him—

"Of what?"

"Of the new opera."

"Ah!—I really don't know; I can't recall what I thought of it just now. The fact is I didn't give much attention to it."

The public seems, by its attitude to the opera, to have simply dismissed it. It is a case of the drum-major who, tired of hearing his virtuosi play—

ra instead of fla

has returned his staff to the minister.

❊ ❊ ❊

Sometimes, however, the public becomes aroused, even passionate; and then it gives vent with fury to its prepossessions, prejudices and infatuations. At the first representation of "Hernani," by Victor Hugo, at the moment when the hero cries:

O viellard stupide! il l'aime!

a "classic," jumping up with indignation exclaimed:

"Is it possible that an old 'as-de-pique' should trifle with the public to this extent?"

Whereupon, a "romantic," who had also heard, replied, with equal indignation—

"You old 'as-de-pique,' what is wrong? That is magnificent. That is really nature, taken from the very life; old 'as-de-pique.' Bravo! Superb!"

There you have it; for music is judged at the theatre in precisely the same way.

XIV

THE SYMPHONIES OF H. REBER

AND

STEPHEN HELLER'S PIANOFORTE WORKS

IN these days of comic-operas, operettas, drawing-
room operas, operas for the open air, as well as
music upon the water—in short, of *useful* works
destined to afford consolation, after daily labour, for
people who are fatigued with making money, it is un-
doubtedly a singular idea to occupy oneself with a
composer of symphonies. But the idea which the composer himself must have had in writing his symphonies
is much more singular still; for, in France, where can
work of this kind ultimately lead a musician? I am
afraid to think of it. The following is, in general,
what happens to an artist who has the misfortune to
yield to the temptation of producing works of this
description. If he has ideas (and, otherwise, he could
never write pure music with no words to suggest imitation, phrases or conventional melodic designs, and

with no accessory of any kind to amuse the eyes of the listener)—well, if he has ideas, he must spend a considerable time in selecting them, putting them in order and examining their value. He then makes a choice; developing with all his art those which have appeared to him the most striking and the most worthy to figure in his musical picture.

We see him now at work, earnestly engaged in weaving his musical fabric. His imagination becomes illumined, his heart is overflowing, and he falls into strange distractions. When he has worked all day, and, at a late hour of the evening, he feels the necessity of breathing the air, he is likely enough to go out with a lighted candle instead of a hat. He lies down, but he cannot sleep; because the harmonious people of his orchestra engage within his brain in diversions which are irreconcilable with repose. It is then that he discovers his boldest and newest combinations, invents original phrases and imagines contrasts the most impossible to foresee. That is the time of veritable inspiration; though occasionally that, also, of deception. If, in fact, after having had a beautiful idea, after having regarded it from every aspect and considered it at leisure, he should have the weakness to rely upon his memory and go to sleep, postponing the question of writing it until the next day, it will nearly always happen that, on waking, all remembrance of the beautiful idea will have disappeared.

The unfortunate composer then experiences a torture which we will not attempt to describe. He tries to recall the melodic or harmonic phantom, the apparition of which has so charmed him; but in vain. Should he succeed in recalling some stray features of it, they lack connection; and seem to be rather the result of a nightmare than of a poetic dream.

"Oh! that sleep! If I had got up to write," he says to himself, "the phantom would not have escaped me; but it is a fatality, and I will think of it no more, but go out."

There he is, walking along quietly, at some distance from his house, not thinking of his symphony, but carelessly humming, as he looks at the water of the river running along, and as he follows with his glance the capricious flight of the birds; when, all at once, the movement of his steps coinciding by chance with the rhythm of the musical phrase that he had forgotten, this phrase comes back to him and he recognises it.

"Ah! how fortunate!" he cries, "there it is. This time, I shall not lose it."

He rapidly passes his hands over his pockets. Horror! He has neither album nor pencil; and it is, therefore, impossible to write. He sings the phrase for fear of forgetting it; and keeps on singing it, changing his course to return home. He upsets the passersby, causes himself to be roughly spoken to, and, after quickening his pace to an extent to cause the dogs to bark at him, at last arrives; still humming, and with a mad look which frightens the house-porter. He opens the door of his apartment, seizes a sheet of paper, writes the cursed phrase with a trembling hand, and sinks down; overcome with fatigue and anxiety, but full of joy, for the idea is his, he has caught it by its wings.

We must recognise that the majority of composers are, as it were, only the secretaries of a sort of musical hobgoblin that they carry within them, and who dictates his thoughts to them whenever he pleases; and whose silence is not to be conquered by the most ardent solicitations when once he has resolved to keep it. Hence, the numerous caprices of thought; hence, those moments when the secretary seems unable to write with sufficient swiftness; and hence, also, those other moments when the hobgoblin seems to be making fun of him by only dictating to him nonsense which is not worth confiding to paper.

I remember that, having taken into my head to compose a cantata with choruses on the little poem of Béranger entitled "Le Cinq Mai," I alighted easily enough upon music for the first two lines; but I stopped short at the last two; which are the most important, because they form the refrain for all the verses:

> Pauvre soldat, je reverrai la France,
> La main d'un fils me fermera les yeux.*

---

* Poor soldier, I shall yet see France again,
  A son's dear hand e'en yet shall close my eyes.

I tried in vain during several weeks to find a suitable melody for this refrain; but all I discovered was mere banality, without either style or expression. At last, I gave it up; and the composition of the cantata was, therefore, abandoned. Two years after that, not thinking of it any more, I was taking a walk in Rome, one day, on a steep bank of the Tiber, which they call the *promenade du Poussin*; when, having approached too closely to the edge, the ground slipped under my foot, and I fell into the river. In falling, the idea that I was about to be drowned, passed through my mind; but perceiving, after my fall, that I should be quit of it with no worse consequences than a foot bath; and that I had simply fallen into the mud, I came out of the Tiber singing:

Pauvre soldat, je reverrai la France,

precisely upon the phrase so vainly and industriously sought two years before.

"Ah!" I cried, "there you are. Better late than never!" and so the cantata was finished.

I now return to my symphonist. Let us suppose his work finished. He then reads it over, and finds that it is good; from which moment he is haunted by the idea of having the parts copied; to which, after more or less resistance, he gives way. He therefore spends, for the parts, a rather considerable sum; but, after all, we must sow—or we cannot reap. Now, we must look for an opportunity to get the new symphony performed; and there are always musical societies possessing a valiant orchestra, which is quite capable of well executing such works. Alas! the occasion perhaps will never come. The symphony is not asked for; if the author proposes it, it is not accepted, it being found too difficult, and the time lacking to study it properly. But, even if it can be well rehearsed and executed properly, the public find it so severe in style that they do not understand it. And, even if the public give it a good reception, two days afterwards it is nevertheless forgotten; and the composer remains " Gros-Jean," as he was before. If he decides to give a concert, it is worse still; for he has to bear enormous expenses for the hall, the executants, the bills, etc.; and, beyond that, pay a considerable tax to the government. His symphony, after having been once heard, is soon forgotten; and he has simply given himself infinite trouble and lost much money.

If he now proposes to a publisher to issue his work, the man of business will look at him astonished, wondering whether he is mad; and reply :

"We have many important things to publish just now; there is so little sale for orchestral music; we cannot; etc." But, possibly, some bold editor may intervene, who believes in the future of the composer, and who is willing to run the risk in order to save a beautiful work from oblivion. The editor's name may be Brandus or Richaut; and he publishes the symphony; he saves it; it will not altogether perish; it will be placed in ten or twelve European musical libraries; five or six devoted artists will buy it; some country philharmonic society will strangle it some day; and then—and then—well, that's all!

The above causes, no doubt, account for the number of new symphonies growing less and less. Haydn wrote more than a hundred; Mozart left seventeen; Beethoven nine; Mendelssohn three; Schubert one; so that M. Reber has had rather more courage than the latter, since he has written four; which the honourable publisher, Richaut, has just published in full score. They are symphonies in the classic form adopted by Haydn and Mozart, each being composed of four movements; an allegro, an adagio, a scherzo or minuet and a finale in quick movement. We must, however, notice the diversity of character of the third movements of these four symphonies. That of the first (in D minor) is a scherzo in duple time; quick, light and sparkling; in the style of those of Mendelssohn. In the second (in C) the scherzo is replaced by a more rapid movement in triple time, partaking of the character of the minuets of Mozart and Haydn. The minuet of the third (in E flat) is, on the contrary, a stately dance; which, in style and movement, is precisely that of the original specimens of this kind of air. The fourth symphony (in G) has, for its third movement, a scherzo in rapid triple time; like the scherzi of Beethoven. Thus, M. Reber, in his symphonies, has given us samples of the different kinds of third movements adopted, successively, by the four great masters—Haydn, Mozart, Beethoven and Mendelssohn. He has, moreover, restored to the symphony (and we congratulate him) the slow—that is the *true* minuet; which differs essentially from the quick minuet of Haydn and Mozart, and of which that in "Armide," by Gluck, will remain the admirable model. The story is told apropos of this piece that Vestris, having said to Gluck at one of the general rehearsals of "Armide":

"Well, chevalier, have you written my minuet?" Gluck replied:

"Yes, but it is in a style so grand that you will be obliged to dance it in the 'Place du Carrousel.'"

The melodic style of M. Reber is always distinguished and pure; and, in some portions of his trios for piano and stringed instruments, he even tends a little to archaism, in such a way as to recall the forms of old masters, such as Rameau, Couperin, etc., but with an amplitude and richness of development which those masters never knew. In his symphonies he is more modern. His harmony is bolder than that of Haydn and Mozart; but this does not imply the least leaning either to the ferocious discords or the cacophonic style systematically adopted, during the last four or five years, by some German musicians who can scarcely be quite sane, and who at this moment are looked upon with apprehension and horror by musical civilisation at large.

L

As to the instrumentation of his symphonies it is careful, delicate, often ingenious and always free from coarseness. The individual parts are designed with precision and exquisite skill. The composition of his orchestra is the same as that of Mozart; the more sonorous instruments such as trombones being excluded; the percussion instruments being restricted to kettledrums and the more modern wind instruments being dispensed with. It is unnecessary to add that the hand of the skilful contrapuntist is everywhere evident, and that the various orchestral parts cross and either pursue or imitate one another with an ease and liberty of manner which are never the cause of any blemish to the ensemble. Finally, it seems to me that one of the most striking merits of M. Reber consists in the general disposition of his movements, in the management of the effects and in that art which is so rare—the art of stopping in time. Without confining himself within mean outlines he never exceeds the point to which the listener may be trusted to follow him without fatigue, and he seems to have Boileau's aphorism continually in mind:

Qui ne sut se borner ne sut jamais écrire.*

I do not know whether the whole of the four symphonies of M. Reber have been performed at the concerts of the Conservatoire; but I heard two of them

---

* Who knew not when to stop, knew never how to write.

a few years ago, at those solemnities to which it is so difficult to gain admission, and both of them obtained a brilliant success.

* * *

Stephen Heller also appears to me to belong to that small, resigned family of musicians who love and respect their art. He has great talent, a keen intelligence, an inexhaustible patience, and convictions which his daily studies and observations, combined with good sense, render unassailable. He is a most skilful pianist; but he never plays in public, and therefore does not exploit the works which he writes for his instrument. For the same reason he has no need to give them the brilliant aspect or the flat and vulgar facility upon which success for the greater part of works written as drawing-room pieces depends. Neither do his productions, in which all the resources of modern pianistic art are employed, present that forbidding appearance which promotes the sale of certain studies to people unable to play four bars of them; but who like to have them lying upon their piano, in order to give the impression that they are able to do so. Heller cannot be reproached with any of this quackery. He has even discontinued giving lessons; thus sacrificing the advantage of having pupils to spread his fame; which is one of greater value than is generally imagined. He writes, tranquilly and when he chooses, beautiful works; these being rich in ideas and generally of a suave colouring; though frequently also full of life. His writings circulate gradually in all places where the art of the piano is cultivated seriously; his reputation increases, and he lives in peace; scarcely deigning to smile at the absurdities of the musical world. Oh! too happy man!

XV

"ROMEO AND JULIET"

Its first representation at the Opera, and first appearances of Madame Vestvali

THERE exist at the present moment five operas of this name; for each one of which the immortal drama of Shakespeare is supposed to have furnished the subject. Nothing, however, could less resemble the masterpiece of the English poet than the libretti, mostly distorted and mean, and sometimes even silly to the point of imbecility, which various composers have set to music. All the librettists, however, pretend that they have been inspired by Shakespeare; and that their torches have been fired at his sun of love. And pale torches they are; for three of them are scarcely little rose-coloured candles; one casts only a little gleam with its smoke; and the last can only be compared to the candle-end of a rag-picker.

What these fabricators of libretti, both French and Italian (with the exception of M. Romani, who is, I believe, the author of the text of Bellini's work) have made of the Shakespearean tragedy surpasses all that can be imagined in the way of puerility and nonsense. I am not assuming that it is possible to transform any given drama into an opera without modifying and disturbing it—even spoiling it, to some extent. I know that. But there are so many intelligent ways of performing this operation, the damaging character of which is rendered unavoidable by the exigencies of the music.

For instance, while recognising the inadvisibility of retaining the whole of the original characters, why has it never occurred to the authors of any of these libretti to retain, at least, one of the personages which are generally suppressed? In the two French operas, which are being played at theatres generally devoted to comic-opera, why have they not inclined to allow either Mercutio or the Nurse to appear; these being two characters so different from the principals that they would have given the musician occasion for striking contrasts in his score? On the other hand, in these two productions of such unequal merit, several new personages are introduced. We find in them, for example, an Antonio, an Alberti, a Cébas, a Gennaro, an Adriani, a Nisa, a Cécile, etc. But for what purpose? To arrive at what results?

In both French operas the conclusions are happy.

At the time of their appearance sad conclusions were out of favour at all our lyric theatres; and the spectacle of death had been forbidden, on account of the extreme sensibility of the public. In the three Italian operas, on the contrary, the final catastrophe of the original is admitted. Romeo poisons himself; Juliet stabs herself with a pretty little gilt dagger; she seats herself comfortably upon the stage by the side of the body of Romeo; draws a tasty little "Ah!" which is supposed to be her last sigh; and there you are!

It must be understood that neither the French nor the Italians, any more than the English themselves, at those of their theatres which are consecrated to the legitimate drama, have ventured to preserve the character of Romeo in its integrity, and to allow his first love for Rosaline even to be suspected. For shame, indeed! To suppose that the young Montague could possibly have already loved any other than a daughter of the Capulets! This would have been altogether unworthy of the conception of this model lover; and would have cancelled the poetry of his character *in toto*; especially in the estimation of a public composed entirely of souls whom we know to be all so essentially constant and pure!

And yet, how profound is the lesson which the poet desired to give! How often do we imagine we love before understanding the nature of the real passion! How many Romeos have died without ever knowing it? How many others have felt their hearts bleed through the long years for a Rosaline separated from their soul, by gulfs, the depths of which they dared not contemplate? How many of them have said to a friend:

> " Tut, I have lost myself; I am not here;
> This is not Romeo, he's some other where."
>
> *   *   *   *   *   *   *
>
> " Farewell: thou canst not teach me to forget."

How often has the lover of Rosaline heard Mercutio say to him:

> " Come, we will draw thee from the mire of love
> Wherein thou stickst up to the ears—"

and has replied only by a smile of incredulity to the joyous philosopher; who could only depart, in weariness at his friend's sadness, saying to himself:

> ' That pale, hard-hearted wench—that Rosaline
> Torments him so that he will sure run mad."

How often has all this continued until, amidst the splendours of the festival given by the rich Capulet, Romeo, at last, perceives his Juliet; a few sounds of whose voice suffice to reveal to him the being of his dreams—to cause his heart to swell and bound under the influence of poetic flame; and his Rosaline's image to vanish, as instantly as that of a ghost at sunrise! And, after the festival, wandering in love round Capulet's house, the prey to divine anguish, and foreseeing the immense revolution which is about to take place in his heart, he hears the avowal of the noble girl, he

trembles with amazement and joy. Then it is that we
have that immortal dialogue worthy of the very angels
in heaven :

<blockquote>

JULIET :

"I gave my heart before thou didst request it :
And yet I would it were to give again.

ROMEO :

Would'st thou withdraw it? for what purpose, love?

JULIET :

But to be frank, and give it thee again.

ROMEO :

O blessed, blessed night ! I am afeard,
Being in night, all this is but a dream,
Too flattering-sweet to be substantial."

</blockquote>

But the time comes for them to part; when, under
the stress of an intense grief, Romeo gives way to
rhapsody. He cannot conceive their being separated,
or understand why anything should intervene between
them. Every sound he hears seems like a cry proceeding from his own breast; and, in the very lights
of heaven, he perceives a fairy illumination expressly
to celebrate their love. The tears of Juliet are her
only reply; for, when once so great a love is born, it is
immense and inexpressible; armed with every power
of imagination, and eternal. It is *eternal*, for the
reason that Romeo and Juliet still live and love as in
the days of Shakespeare; but, when this sublime poem
is compared with the grotesque libretti called
"operas" which have been based upon it; when it is
confronted with these icy rhapsodies which seem to

have been written with cucumber-juice and nenuphar, the feeling which arises in the breast of all who know the original work is one of thankfulness that the divine Shakespeare is beyond the reach of such outrage.

Of the five operas to which I referred at the beginning, the "Romeo" of Steibelt, represented for the first time at the Théâtre-Feydeau, on September 10, 1793, is immensely superior to the others. It is, at least, a score; and really does exist, as a work. It possesses style, sentiment and invention; besides novelties of harmony and instrumentation which are really remarkable; and which, at the period of the production of this work, must have appeared excessively bold. Besides a well-designed overture, full of pathetic and energetic features, there is a very beautiful air preceded by recitative:

Du calme de la nuit tout ressent les doux charmes,.

the andante of which is of a melodic turn which is both expressive and distinguished. In it the composer has had the incredible audacity to finish upon the third of the key, without rehashing the final cadence; as was the custom with the majority of his contemporaries.

The subject of this air is that of the second scene of the third act of Shakespeare's "Romeo"; where Juliet, who has just been married, is alone in her chamber; waiting for her young husband.

" Spread thy close curtain, love-performing night !
That, runaway's eyes may wink ; and Romeo
Leap to these arms, untalk'd of and unseen !—
Lovers can see to do their amorous rites
By their own beauties ; or, if love be blind,
It best agrees with night—come, civil night,
Thou sober-suited matron, all in black,
And learn me how to lose a winning match."

We must also mention, in connection with Steibelt's
work, an air of old Capulet with chorus, which is
characterised by a peculiar wildness.

"Oui, la fureur de se venger
Est un premier besoin de l'âme !"

Also, the funeral march :

" Grâces, vertus, soyez en deuil !"

and the air of Juliet when she is about to take the
sleeping-draught. It is dramatic, and even highly
emotional; but what a distance (ye gods!) between
this musical inspiration, however well graduated may
be its interest right up to the end, and the prodigious
crescendo of Shakespeare's work. Shakespeare was,
indeed, the true inventor of the *crescendo* ; and his application of it in this instance is without a parallel
anywhere; unless it may be in the fourth scene of Act
III of "Hamlet" : at the words :

" Now, mother, what's the matter?"

what a rising tide of terror is that presented by the
following long monologue of Juliet :

" What if it be a poison, which the friar
Subtly hath minister'd to have me dead;
Lest in this marriage he should be dishonour'd,
Because he married me before to Romeo?
I fear it is: and yet, methinks, it should not,
For he hath still been tried a holy man:
How if, when I am laid into the tomb,
I wake before the time that Romeo
Come to redeem me? there's a fearful point!
Shall I not then be stifled in the vault,
To whose foul mouth no healthsome air breathes in,
And there die strangled ere my Romeo comes?
Or, if I live, is it not very like,
The horrible conceit of death and night,
Together with the terror of the place—
As in a vault, an ancient receptacle,
Where, for these many hundred years, the bones
Of all my buried ancestors are pack'd;
Where bloody Tybalt, yet but green in earth,
Lies fest'ring in his shroud; where, as they say,
At some hours in the night spirits resort;—
Alack, alack! it is not like, that I,
So early waking—what with loathsome smells;
And shrieks like mandrakes' torn out of the earth,
That living mortals, hearing them, run mad;—
O! if I wake, shall I not be distraught,
Environed with all these hideous fears?
And madly play with my forefathers' joints?
And pluck the mangled Tybalt from his shroud?
And, in this rage, with some great kinsman's bone,
As with a club, dash out my desperate brains?
O, look! methinks I see my cousin's ghost
Seeking out Romeo, that did spit his body
Upon a rapier's point: stay, Tybalt, stay!—
Romeo, Romeo, Romeo, I drink to thee."

I quite believe it to be within the power of music to
rise to this height of expression; but I am sadly afraid

that it has never yet done so. In listening, at the representation, to these terrible scenes, my very brain seems to turn in my head, and my very bones to crack in my flesh; whilst the prodigious cry of love and anguish which I once heard is one which I can never forget:

> Romeo, Romeo, Romeo, I drink to thee!

*   *   *

How absurd to think that, after having known such works and experienced such impressions, one can take your paltry luke-warm passions and your affections, the duration of whose warmth is as that of sealing-wax, in anything like a serious manner! How absurd to think that those who have lived all their life in countries to which these great Oceanic lakes of art belong—in countries where these proud and flourishing virgin-forests of art are native, can accommodate themselves to your little flower-gardens with their borders of square-cut box; to your globes where the little red fishes swim; or to your pools which are merely the haunt of toads! Ye miserable concoctors of microscopic opera!

*   *   *

The other French score bearing the title of "Romeo and Juliet" is scarcely known nowadays; and, unfortunately for our national amour-propre, is by Dalayrac. The author of this abominable libretto had just enough sense not to give his name. The whole is miserable, flat and stupid in every conceivable respect;

giving the impression of a work composed by two idiots who knew nothing about passion, sentiment, good sense, their native language, *or* music.

But, in these two operas, the part of Romeo is, at least, written for a man. The three Italian masters, on the contrary, have chosen that the lover of Juliet should be represented by a woman; this being a relic of the ancient musical manners of the Italian school, and a result of constant preoccupation about a childish sensualism. Women were preferred for the parts of lovers because, in duets, two feminine voices more easily produce those successions of thirds which are so dear to Italian ears. In the old operas of this school there are scarcely any bass parts to be found; low voices being disliked by this public of sybarites, who were attracted by sweet sonorities as children are by lollipops.

The opera of Zingarelli enjoyed a rather long popularity, both in France and Italy. Its music is tranquil and graceful and contains neither any trace of the Shakespearean characters nor any more pretension to express their passions than if the composer had not understood a word of the language to which he adapted his melodies. An air of Romeo is still quoted called :

Ombra adorata,''

which was so celebrated as, for a long time, to suffice to draw the public to the Théâtre-Italien, and to cause it to put up with all the tiresomeness of the rest of

the work. This piece is graceful, elegant and very
well disposed, upon the whole; and, in it, the flute
especially figures with some pretty passages, happily
arranged in dialogue with fragments of the vocal
phrase. Everything approaches cheerfulness in this
air; and Romeo, who is about to die, dwells especially
upon the delight of rejoining Juliet above; and of enjoying, with her, the pure delights of love in a celestial
home:

> " Nel fortunato Eliso
> Avra contenti il cor."

Some of Juliet's pieces are strangely mixed up with
truthful accents and clownish traits. In one grand
air, for instance, she pathetically exclaims that no soul
is to be found so overwhelmed with woe as hers:

> " Non v'é un alma a questo eccesso
> Sventurata al par di me."

Then, reflecting for a moment, she starts off *con brio*;
and vocalises *without any words* a long series of trip-
lets, of most joyful effect, the playfulness of which is
further increased by that of the first violins playing
scherzo-like figures.

As to the final duo, at the terrible scene, in which
Juliet (who believed that she had arrived at perfect
happiness) learns that Romeo is poisoned, is present at
his agony, and, lastly, dies upon his body, nothing
could be more calm than all this anguish; and nothing
more charming than these convulsions. Now or never
we may say with Hamlet:

"No, no, they do but jest, poison in jest; no offence i' the world."

Of the "Romeo" of Vaccaï scarcely more is now performed than the third act; but this is generally cited as full of passion and beautiful dramatic colour, though I must confess that, having heard it in London, I could find no trace of those qualities; as the two lovers, in their desperation, behave, there also, with extreme calm; in short they "do but jest, poison in jest." I do not know whether it is true that this third act now forms the fourth of Bellini's opera just represented; at all events, I have not recognised it. It was said, a few weeks ago, that the last act of Bellini was too weak; the poisoning in it being again too much "in jest." It must be so, indeed; for I heard it in Florence twenty-five years ago and cannot remember anything about it.

This "Romeo," fifth of the name, although one of the most indifferent of Bellini's scores, contains some pretty things; including a finale full of impulse, in which there is a beautiful phrase, sung in unison by the two lovers, which is well displayed. This passage struck me the very first time I heard it, at the theatre of the Pergola; being there well rendered in every way. There were the two lovers who had been forcibly separated by their furious parents, the Montagues, retaining Romeo, and the Capulets Juliet; in spite of which, at the last return of the beautiful phrase:

" Nous nous reverrons au ciel?"

they escape from the hands of their respective perse-
cutors and rush into one another's arms with genuine
Shakespearean fury. Just then we began really to
think they were in love; but great care has been exercised at the Opera not to risk such boldness, as it is
not considered decent in France for two theatrical lovers
to embrace with such abandonment. It is not suitable.

As far as I remember, the gentle Bellini has only employed a moderate instrumentation, without either side
or bass-drums; although, at the Opera, his orchestra
was provided with those auxiliaries. Considering that
there are scenes of civil war in the course of the drama,
it is doubtful if the orchestra can dispense with side-
drum; besides which it is scarcely now possible to
sing or dance without a bass-drum accompaniment.
However, at the moment when Juliet drags herself to
the feet of her father with cries of despair, the strong
beats of the bar are struck so imperturbably and with
such pompous regularity by the bass-drum as to produce, it must be confessed, an effect of the most irre-
sistibly comic description. The drum-strokes, being
heard above everything, naturally monopolise attention; so that no further respect is paid to Juliet, but
an impression is produced akin to that we should receive from a military band marching at the head of a
legion of the national guard. The dances included in
Bellini's score have no great value, as they lack spirit
and charm. There is an andante, however, which is

M

enjoyable; that, namely, which is based upon an air
of "La Straniera," entitled:

"Meco tu vieni ô misera,"

one of the most touching of all Bellini's inspirations.
It may be astonishing that they dance to it; but what
will you? We dance to everything now; we *do* anything *on* anything.

The costumes have no particular feature; that of
Lorenzo being the only one that has courted attention,
consisting of an overcoat furred with marten. Good
Lorenzo is dressed up like a Pole; the presumption
being that it must have been rather cold at Verona at
that time. Marié, who played this "fur" part, had a
cold; which occasioned him several vocal accidents.
Gueymard makes a very energetic Tybalt; Madame
Gueymard rendering the part of Juliet most musically,
with her golden voice. Madame Vestvali, the debu-
tante, is a tall and beautiful woman, with a low con-
tralto voice of extended compass, but lacking brilliancy in its middle register. Her vocalisation is
rather laboured; and her attack, especially in the upper octave, occasionally fails in purity of intonation.
She played Romeo with much—well, "dignity."

The tomb scene, as played by great English artists,
will remain a sublime marvel of dramatic art. At the
name of Romeo, escaping feebly from the lips of the
reviving Juliet, the young Montague, struck with
stupor, stands motionless for a moment. A second

and more tender appeal attracts his attention to the monument; when a movement by Juliet dissipates all doubt. At the thought—

"She lives!"

he rushes forward towards the funereal couch; he seizes the adored body; he tears its veil aside; and, sustaining it upright in his arms, he rushes forward. Juliet raises her dim eyes towards him; he frantically addresses her; presses her in a close embrace; pushes aside the hair which falls upon her forehead; covers her face with feverish kisses; and then breaks into convulsive laughter, for, in the delirium of his joy, he has forgotten that he is about to die. Juliet breathes! Oh Juliet! Juliet!

But a frightful warning pain soon brings him to his senses. The poison he has taken is even now doing its work—even now it is gnawing at his entrails, and he must die!

"O potent poison!
Capulet! Capulet! mercy!"

He thinks he sees the father of Juliet coming to take her from him once more; and thus moves forward on his knees, delirious.

The form assumed by the above scene in the new opera is as follows:

Steps are arranged on each side of the tomb of Juliet, in order to enable her to descend commodiously and decently. This takes place; and, with measured steps, she advances towards her motionless lover. Thereupon, they proceed to entertain one another quite tranquilly about their little affairs :

ROMEO : Que vois-je !
JULIET :   . . . . Romeo !
ROMEO :   . . . . Juliette vivante !
JULIET : D'une morte apparente
             Le réveil *en ce jour*
             A ton amour va donc me rendre.
ROMEO : Dis-tu vrai?
JULIET :   . . . . Lorenzo n'a-t-il pu te l'apprendre
ROMEO : Sans rien savoir, sans rien comprendre
             J'ai cru pour mon malheur te perdre sans retour.*

*   *   *

"Are there no stones in heaven?"†

No : Othello's question is idle, and there are none. No : there is no beautiful or ugly, no true or false, no sublime or absurd; everything is on one level. The public should know; they who are such models of impassable indifference.

But let us be calm. From the point of view of the art (nothing to do with *art*) of making money, the belief is that, in engaging Madame Vestvali, and in mounting Bellini's "Romeo," the direction of the grand Opera has made a bad stroke of business.

Let me sleep !
I can no more !

---

* As the worthlessness of this text has caused Berlioz to quote it only in derision, translation is unnecessary.

† The measure of Berlioz's indignation may be gathered from these lines being given in English : the language of Shakespeare being evidently chosen with intention for the expression of his wrath. (Translator's note.)

XVI

ABOUT A FAUST-BALLET

INCLUDING A WITTICISM OF BEETHOVEN

THE idea of making Faust dance is perhaps the most prodigious which has ever entered into the brainless heads of those men-of-every-trade who profane everything without meaning the least harm; just as the blackbirds and sparrows in our public gardens make perches of the finest statuary. The composer of the Faust-ballet seems to me a hundred times more astonishing than Molière's marquis, who was busy writing the entire history of Rome *in madrigals*. As to the musicians who have made the various characters of this celebrated poem sing, they are forgiven much as they have also loved much; besides which, they might plead that, after all, these personages rightly belong to the art of reverie and of passion; to the art of the vague and the infinite; to the immense art of sounds.

With how many dedications has Goethe, the Olympian, been afflicted! How many musicians have addressed him:

"O thou!"

or even, simply:

"O!"

to which he either answered, or should have answered:

"I am very grateful, my dear sir, that you should have condescended to illustrate my poem; which, but for you, might have remained in obscurity"; etc.

He was a wag, this god of Weimar! so inappropriately named by some unknown German Voltaire. Only once did he find his match in a musician; for it seems proved, at last, that musical art is not so degrading as literary folk have for a long time tried to make out; and that, for a century now, at least, it is said that there have been almost as many clever musicians as literary fools.

Well, then, Goethe had come to pass a few weeks at Vienna; for he liked the society of Beethoven, who had just really illustrated his tragedy of "Egmont." Sauntering one day in the Prater with the melancholy Titan, the passers by were bowing with respect to the distinguished pair; though Goethe alone replied to their salutations.

Impatient, at last, on account of being obliged to raise his hand to his hat so frequently, he turned to Beethoven saying:

"These good folk are decidedly fatiguing with their salutes."

"Don't be angry," replied Beethoven quietly, "don't be angry, your Excellence; their salutes are most likely intended for *me*."

XVII

TO BE, OR NOT TO BE

A PARAPHRASE

TO be, or not to be, that is the question. Whether 'tis nobler for a courageous soul to suffer the slings and arrows of bad operas, ridiculous concerts, indifferent virtuosi, and mad composers; or to take arms against this sea of troubles, and by opposing end them?

To die.—To sleep.—No more.—And by a sleep to say we end the ear-torture, the sufferings of heart and mind and the thousand griefs imposed upon our intelligence and common sense by the sort of criticism we see exercised; 'tis a consummation devoutly to be wished.

To die.—To sleep—To sleep, and have the nightmare perhaps; aye, there's the rub. For in that sleep of death what dreams may come when we have shuffled off this mortal coil, what mad theories we may have to examine; what discordant scores we may have to listen to; what idiots we may have to praise; what outrages we may see inflicted upon masterpieces; what extravagances we may hear preached; or what windmills we may see taken for giants!

Here have we ample food for reflection; for it is this thought which both renders *feuilletons* so numerous and prolongs the existence of the unfortunates who write them.

For who, in fact, would bear the obligation of living in an insensate world; the continual spectacle of its madness; the inappreciation and stupid error caused by its ignorance; the injustice of its justice and the icy indifference of those who rule? Who would enter the whirlpool of ignoble passion; or of mean interest, taking the name of love of art? Who would lower themselves to the level of discussing the absurd; of being a soldier, under generals who require to be taught the elements of military science; or, of being a traveller, under guides who know nothing of the course to be taken; and who wander from it, even after it has been pointed out to them? Who would suffer all this, when deliverance from such humiliation could be so easily compassed by a flask of chloroform or a revolver? Who would resign themselves, in this weary world, to witness despair where hope had been; lassitude born of inaction; or anger the outcome of patience exhausted? but that the dread of something after death, that undiscovered country from whose bourne no critic e'er returns, puzzles the will:

Enough! for it is not even open to us to meditate.

But soft! Here comes the young singer, Ophelia, carrying a score, and feigning a smile.

"What do you require of me? Flatteries of course; always flatteries."

"My lord, I have a score of yours that I have longèd long to redeliver; I pray you now receive it."

"No, no; I never gave you aught."

"My honour'd lord I know right well you did; and with it words of so sweet breath composed as made the thing more rich: its perfume lost, take it again; for to the noble mind, rich gifts wax poor when givers prove unkind. There my lord."

"Ha, ha! are you honest?"

"My lord?"

"And you are a singer?"

"What means your lordship?"

"That if you be honest, and at the same time a singer by profession, your honesty should admit no discourse to your profession."

"Could art, my lord, have better commerce than with honesty?"

"Ay truly; for the power of your talent will sooner transform honesty from what it is to a bawd, than the force of honesty can translate talent into his likeness: this was some time a paradox, but now the time gives it proof. I did admire you once."

"Indeed, my lord, you made me believe so."

"You should not have believed me; my admiration was not real."

"I was the more deceived."

"Get thee to a nunnery; what is your ambition? A celebrated name, plenty of money, the applause of fools, a titled husband and the name of duchess. Yes, yes; they all dream of marrying a prince. Why wouldst thou be a breeder of idiots?"

"Oh help him, you sweet heavens?"

"If thou dost marry, I'll give thee this plague for thy dowry : let a woman who is an artiste be as chaste as ice, as pure as snow, she shall not escape calumny. Get thee to a nunnery, go; farewell : or, if thou wilt needs marry, marry a fool; for wise men know well enough what monsters you make of them. To a nunnery go; and quickly too. Farewell."

"O heavenly powers, restore him."

"I have heard of your vocal coquetries too, of your ridiculous pretentions, and of your vanity. God hath given you one voice and you make yourselves another. A masterpiece is confided to you and you disfigure it; you change its character ; you load it with miserable ornaments; you make insolent cuts in it, introducing grotesque passages, ridiculous arpeggios and comical trills; you insult not only the master, but art, good sense and all people of taste. I say we will have no more. To a nunnery, go !" *(Exit.)*

The youthful Ophelia is not altogether wrong, and Hamlet may have lost his head a little; though that is not likely to be noticed in a musical world where all the rest are absolutely mad. Moreover, this unfortunate prince of Denmark has also his lucid moments; and, in fact, is only mad when the wind blows from the north-west. When the wind is in the south, he can very well distinguish an eagle from a buzzard.

XVIII

THE "LITTLE DOG" SCHOOL

THE "little dog" school is that of singers whose voices are possessed of an extraordinary extension of the upper portion of their scale; and who, in consequence, are enabled to wind up every cadence with a high E or F. The pleasure which this performance causes to the listener, as well as the nature of its quality of tone, is similar to the pleasure afforded to a little dog when one treads upon its paw and to the *timbre* of his howl.

We must acknowledge, however, that Madame Cabel, at the period of her practising this style of singing, always hit her mark. When she aimed at an E or F, or even a super-high G, it really was an E, F or G which the listener heard; though without being thankful for it.

But her pupils or imitators, as a rule, are not so fortunate. When it is a question of getting E, they generally arrive at D; and when it is a question of getting

F, they generally arrive at E; so that, in their case, the transports of admiration are quite frantic.

This injustice to both the music and its auditor* succeeded, at last, in disgusting Madame Cahel with her school; which was bound to happen. Now, she restricts herself to singing, like the charming woman that she is; and thinks no more of imitating either the birds or the

"little dogs."

---

* Cette *injustice* et cette *injustesse.*

CATALOGUE OF
BOOKS ON MUSIC

Literature covering every branch
of Music, Biographical and Critical
Studies of Composers, Histories of
Musical Instruments, also valuable
Textbooks and Tutors for Teachers
and Students of the Piano, Organ,
Violin, Cello, Theory, Singing, etc.

All prices are net and postage extra

Published by
WILLIAM REEVES Bookseller Limited
1a Norbury Crescent, London, S.W.16

Telephone: POLlards 2108

BOOKS ABOUT MUSIC

ÆSTHETICS OF MUSICAL ART, or The Beautiful in Music. By Dr. FERDINAND HAND. Translated from the German by WALTER E. LAWSON, *Mus.Bac. Cantab, etc.* Third Edition. Crown 8vo, cloth, 16/–.

THE BOWED HARP. A Study of the History of Early Musical Instruments. By OTTO ANDERSSON, *Ph.D., President of the Swedish University at Abo.* From the Original Swedish Edition, revised by the Author. The Translation Edited with additional footnotes by KATHLEEN SCHLESINGER. 116 Illustrations, Bibliography and Index. 340 pages, 8vo, cloth, 35/–.

CATECHISM OF MUSICAL HISTORY AND BIOGRAPHY. With Especial Reference to the English School. By F. J. CROWEST. 187 pages. Post 8vo, cloth, 5/–; paper, 2/6.

CHAMBER MUSIC AND ITS MASTERS IN THE PAST AND IN THE PRESENT. By Dr. N. KILBURN. New Edition, revised, and with additional chapters by GERALD ABRAHAM. With Plates and Music Illustrations. Crown 8vo, cloth, 21/–.

CHRONOMETRICAL CHART OF MUSICAL HISTORY. Presenting a Bird's Eye View from the Pre-Christian Era to the XXth Century. By C. A. HARRIS, *A.R.C.O.*, etc. 5/–

THE DEEPER SOURCES OF THE BEAUTY AND EXPRESSION OF MUSIC. By JOSEPH GODDARD. With many Musical Examples. Crown 8vo, cloth, 10/–.

ELIZABETHAN VIRGINAL MUSIC AND ITS COMPOSERS. By M. H. GLYN. Second Edition, Revised, 1934. Demy 8vo, cloth, 21/–.
The author has studied all virginal manuscripts and collated a considerable part of their contents. A full index of these manuscripts is included, together with detailed references as to where they are located. Besides accounts of the lives of Byrd, Bull, Gibbons and Farnaby, there are notes concerning 26 lesser-known composers for the virginals. An explanation of Elizabethan music terms forms part of the book.

THE GIPSY IN MUSIC. By FRANZ LISZT. Translated by EDWIN EVANS.

> Gipsy and Jew, Two Wandering Races.
> Gipsy Life in Relation to Art.
> Gipsy Music and Musicians.

The result of the Author's long Experience and Investigations of the Gipsies and their Music. With Portraits of the Author etc. Demy 8vo, cloth, 35/–.

HISTORY OF THE HARP. From the Earliest Period. By JOHN THOMAS (*Pencerdd Gwalia*). 8vo, paper covers, 6/-.

HISTORY OF THE TRUMPET OF BACH AND HANDEL. By WERNER MENKE. Translated by GERALD ABRAHAM. 5 Plates and a Supplement of Music. Crown 8vo, cloth, 18/-.

This history of the trumpet from its earliest use as an artistic instrument, gives special reference to its employment by Bach and Handel. The correct modern performance of the old parts is discussed, and a description of a new instrument invented by the author for this purpose is included.

HOW TO LISTEN TO GOOD MUSIC and Encourage the Taste in Instrumental and Vocal Music. With many useful Notes for Listener and Executant. By K. BROADLEY GREENE. Complete, cloth, 8/6, or in two books, paper, 2/6 each.

INTRODUCTORY SKETCH OF IRISH MUSICAL HISTORY. By W. H. GRATTAN FLOOD. A compact Record of the Progress of Music in Ireland during 1,000 Years. Portraits. Crown 8vo, cloth, 10/6.

MUSIC IN THE HIRSCH LIBRARY (Part 53 of the Catalogue of Printed Music in the British Museum), by A. HYATT KING and C. HUMPHRIES, 1951. Published for the Trustees of the British Museum. This catalogue, prepared by the Museum staff, lists also a considerable number of works which were either not included in the original four volume catalogue by P. Hirsch, or were acquired later. 4to, cloth, 42/-.

MUSIC OF THE MOST ANCIENT NATIONS, particularly of the Assyrians, Egyptians and Hebrews, with special reference to Discoveries in Western Asia and Egypt. By CARL ENGEL, 1864 (reprinted 1929). About 100 illustrations and many music examples. Demy 8vo, cloth, 42/-.

MUSICAL DEVELOPMENT, or Remarks on the Spirit of the Principal Musical Forms. An Æsthetical Investigation, in which an Attempt is made to show the Action in Music of certain Laws of Human Expression; to point out what are the Spiritual Aims of the Chief Forms of Composition, and the Broad Principles upon which they should be Constructed. By JOSEPH GODDARD. 8vo, cloth, 10/-.

NATIONAL MUSIC OF THE WORLD. By H. F. CHORLEY.
Edited by H. G. HEWLETT. Many Music Examples. Third
Edition. Crown 8vo, cloth, 15/–.

OPERA STORIES OF TODAY AND YESTERDAY. Retold Act
by Act (including Wagner's Ring). By E. DUNCAN. Crown 8vo,
cloth, 6/6.

PAN PIPES, THE SPIRIT OF MUSIC in Nature, Art and
Legends, from East to West. Sixteen Articles for General
Reading, with Drawings of Eastern Musical Instruments.
By G. P. GREEN. Crown 8vo, cloth, 7/6.

THE PLACE OF SCIENCE IN MUSIC. By H. SAINT-GEORGE.
For Advanced Students of Harmony. With music examples.
8vo, 2/6.

POLISH MUSIC AND CHOPIN, ITS LAUREATE. A His-
torical Account from 995 to the Present Time, including
Chopin and his Works. By E. RAYSON. Four Portraits.
Square 8vo, boards, 6/–; paper covers, 3/6.

RISE AND DEVELOPMENT OF MILITARY MUSIC. By Dr.
H. G. FARMER. With Illustrations of Early Instruments and
Music Examples, and Short Biographical Notices of all the
Staff Bandmasters. Crown 8vo, cloth, 16/–.

RISE AND DEVELOPMENT OF OPERA. Embracing a Com-
parative View of the Art in Italy, Germany, France and
England. By JOSEPH GODDARD. Showing the Cause of the
Falling Back of the English School in the Modern Period, and
the Compensation which that Involved. Numerous Music
Examples, Portraits and Facsimiles. Crown 8vo, cloth, 18/–.

**SOME ASPECTS OF CHINESE MUSIC AND SOME
THOUGHTS AND IMPRESSIONS ON ART PRINCIPLES
IN MUSIC.** By G. P. GREEN. Post 8vo, cloth, 6/–, paper
covers, 3/6.

SOME ASPECTS OF GIPSY MUSIC. By D. C. PARKER. Post
8vo, cloth, 6/–, paper covers, 3/6.

SOME FAMOUS SYMPHONIES, How to Understand Them.
With their Story and Simple Analysis. Numerous Portraits.
By J. F. PORTE. Dealing with Symphonies of Beethoven,
Berlioz, Borodin, Brahms, Chausson, Dvorák, Elgar, César
Franck, Haydn, Mendelssohn, Mozart, Schubert, Stanford
and Tchaïkovsky. Complete in cloth, 8/–, or in 2 separate
parts, paper, 2/6 each.

THE SOURCES OF KEYBOARD MUSIC IN ENGLAND. By CHARLES VAN DEN BORREN, translated by J. E. Matthew. 378 pages, 237 music examples. Crown 8vo, cloth, 21/-.

A standard European work of musical scholarship and one which is of vital interest to all students of keyboard music of the 16th and early 17th centuries.

The collection of keyboard music which naturally provides the basis for this study is the Fitzwilliam Virginal Book, and detailed treatment, copiously illustrated with music examples, is given to the various figures—melodic, rhythmic, and harmonic—in this music and to the forms and styles cultivated by composers for the Virginal. Originally published in England in 1915, this book remains the only thorough study of its type, illuminating a most important branch of English and European music.

TREATISE ON BYZANTINE MUSIC. By S. G. HATHERLEY. 208 Music Examples. 162 pages, 4to, cloth, 25/-.

There are upwards of 50 unabbreviated musical pieces, ancient and modern, from Greek, Russian, Turkish and Egyptian sources, given and fully analysed.

TRIBAL MUSIC AND DANCING IN THE SOUTHERN SUDAN, at Social and Ceremonial Gatherings. A descriptive account of the music, rhythm, etc., from personal observation. By Dr. A. N. TUCKER. 5 illustrations, 61 music examples illustrating the dances, songs and rhythm. 57 pages, demy 8vo, cloth, 10/6.

THE TROUBADOUR AS MUSICIAN, Past and Present. By C. A. HARRIS. 2/6.

THE WORLD'S EARLIEST MUSIC. Traced to its Beginnings in Ancient Lands. By collected Evidences of Relics, Records, History and Musical Instruments, from Greece, Etruria, Egypt, China, through Assyria and Babylonia to the Primitive Home, the Land of Akkad and Sumer. By HERMANN SMITH. With sixty-five Illustrations, nearly 400 pages. Crown 8vo, cloth, 25/-.

BOOKS ABOUT MUSICIANS AND THEIR WORKS

FROM MENDELSSOHN TO WAGNER. Being the Memoirs of J. W. Davison, forty years Music Critic of *The Times*, compiled by his son, HENRY DAVISON, from Memoranda and Documents. With 52 portraits of Musicians and Important Letters (previously unpublished) of Mendelssohn, Berlioz, Gounod, Jullien, Macfarren, Sterndale Bennett, etc. Index, 539 pages, 8vo, cloth, 42/-.

MUSIC AND MUSICIANS. Essays and Criticisms, by ROBERT SCHUMANN. Translated, Edited and Annotated by F. R. RITTER. Two volumes, crown 8vo, cloth, 35/- each.

Schumann's literary gifts and interests almost equalled his musical ones. From boyhood he was drawn to literary expression, and his writings on music belong to the best among the romantic literature of the 19th century. The same fire, poetry, directness of expression, the same inventiveness we love in his compositions, also animates his prose.

MUSICAL MEMORIES. By WILLIAM SPARK, *Mus.Doc.* (*late Organist of the Town Hall, Leeds*). Third Edition. With sixteen Portraits. Thick crown 8vo, cloth, 10/-.

REEVES' DICTIONARY OF MUSICIANS. Biographical Accounts of about 2,500 Noteworthy Musicians of the Past and Present. Edited by EDMUNDSTOUNE DUNCAN and Others. Crown 8vo, cloth, 7/6, paper covers, 4/-.

SKETCHES OF ENGLISH GLEE COMPOSERS. Historical, Biographical and Critical. From about 1735-1866. By D. BAPTIE. Post 8vo, cloth, 10/-.

SOME MUSICAL RECOLLECTIONS OF FIFTY YEARS. By RICHARD HOFFMAN. With Memoir by MRS. HOFFMAN. Illustrated with many Portraits. Crown 8vo, cloth, 10/-.

An interesting book of reminiscences by a prominent Anglo-American pianist and composer (1831-1909). He studied under Pleyel, Moscheles, Rubinstein and Liszt, and became a concert pianist in New York, and also toured with Jenny Lind. Hoffman composed and published many pianoforte pieces of the brilliant kind in vogue at the time.

STUDIES IN RUSSIAN MUSIC. Critical Essays on the most important of Rimsky-Korsakov's operas, Borodin's "Prince Igor," Dargomïzhsky's "Stone Guest," etc.; with chapters on Glinka, Mussorgsky, Balakirev and Tschaïkovsky. By GERALD ABRAHAM. 92 music examples. 350 pages, demy 8vo, cloth, 25/-.

ON RUSSIAN MUSIC. Critical and Historical Studies of Glinka's Operas, Balakirev's Works, etc. With chapters dealing with Compositions by Borodin, Rimsky-Korsakov, Tchaïkovsky, Mussorgsky, Glazunov, and various other Aspects of Russian Music. By GERALD ABRAHAM. With Frontispiece and 88 Music Examples. Demy 8vo, cloth, 21/-.

The above two books complement one another, and together form a valuable survey of Russian music of the period 1836 to 1910. The operas of Rimsky-Korsakov are studied fully, also Borodin's "Prince Igor", Glinka's operas and Balakirev's music. Gerald Abraham is Professor of Music at Liverpool University, and is the chief English authority on Russian music.

THE SYMPHONY WRITERS SINCE BEETHOVEN. Critica Essays on Schubert, Schumann, Götz, Brahms, Tchaïkovsky, Brückner, Berlioz, Liszt, Strauss, Mahler, Mendelssohn, Saint-Saëns, etc. By FELIX WEINGARTNER. Translated by A. BLES. Twelve Portraits. *Second Impression.* With Chapter added by D. C. PARKER on Weingartner's Symphony No. 5. Crown 8vo, cloth, 16/-.

WITH THE GREAT COMPOSERS. A Series of Pen Pictures, exhibiting in the form of Interviews the Personal Characteristics as Artists of the World's great Tone Poets. By GERALD CUMBERLAND. Portraits. Cr. 8vo, cloth, 10/-.

Deals with Chopin, Haydn, Mendelssohn, Paganini, Beethoven, Handel, Rossini, Schubert, Liszt, Berlioz, Mozart, Wagner Tchaïkovsky, Cherubini, Wolf, Borodin, Schumann, Sullivan.

HOW TO PLAY BACH'S 48 PRELUDES AND FUGUES. A Guide Book for the use of Piano Students as an aid to the Unravelling and Interpretation of these Masterpieces, ensuring a more Intelligent Keyboard Rendering. By C. W. WILKINSON. Crown 8vo, cloth, 10/-.

BALFE, HIS LIFE AND WORK. By WM. ALEXANDER BARRETT. Over 300 pages. Crown 8vo, cloth, 21/-.

BEETHOVEN. By RICHARD WAGNER. With a Supplement from the Philosophical Works of Arthur Schopenhauer. Translated by EDWARD DANNREUTHER. Third Edition. Crown 8vo, cloth, 18/-.

BEETHOVEN AND HIS PIANO WORKS (Sonatas, Concertos, Variations, etc.). Descriptive and Analytic Aid to their Understanding and Rendering. By HERBERT WESTERBY. With list of Principal Editions and Bibliography. 3 illustrations, 45 music examples. Crown 8vo, cloth, 10/-.

BEETHOVEN'S PIANOFORTE SONATAS Explained for the Lovers of the Musical Art. By ERNST VON ELTERLEIN. Translated by E. HILL, with Preface by ERNST PAUER. Revised Edition (the Seventh issue). With Portrait, and View of Beethoven's House. Crown 8vo, cloth, 10/-.

NOTES ON THE INTERPRETATION OF 24 FAMOUS PIANO SONATAS BY BEETHOVEN. By J. ALFRED JOHNSTONE. Portrait, crown 8vo, cloth, 12/6.

BEETHOVEN'S PIANO SONATAS. A Descriptive Commentary on the Sonatas in the light of Schnabel's Interpretations; giving an æsthetic Appreciation of each Sonata, with an Outline of the Development of the Sonata Form in Beethoven's hands. With a Biographical Sketch of Schnabel and an account of his activity as an executant, composer and teacher. By RUDOLF KASTNER. Translated by GERALD ABRAHAM. 55 pages, post 8vo, paper, 3/6.

A CRITICAL STUDY OF BEETHOVEN'S NINE SYMPHONIES, with a Few Words on His Trios and Sonatas, a Criticism of "Fidelio" and an Introductory Essay on Music. By HECTOR BERLIOZ. Translated from the French by EDWIN EVANS. Portrait. Crown 8vo, cloth, 21/-.

BEETHOVEN'S NINE SYMPHONIES Fully Described and Analysed. A complete Account of Thematic Material and auxiliary Motives, an Analytical Chart of each Movement, full Technical Descriptions of Developments, Particulars of Formal and Rhythmic Features, Epitomical Tables, etc. Illustrated by 637 Musical Examples. By EDWIN EVANS. Cloth, Vol. I (Nos. 1 to 5), 21/-. Vol. II (Nos. 6 to 9), out of print.

BEETHOVEN'S SYMPHONIES Critically Discussed by ALEXANDER TEETGEN. With Preface by JOHN BROADHOUSE. Second Edition. Post 8vo, cloth, 6/6.

THE CRITICAL WRITINGS OF HECTOR BERLIOZ

A CRITICAL STUDY OF BEETHOVEN'S NINE SYM-PHONIES, with a few Words on his Trios and Sonatas, and a Criticism of Fidelio. Portrait. Crown 8vo, cloth, 21/-.

GLUCK AND HIS OPERAS, with an Account of their Relation to Musical Art. Portrait. Crown 8vo, cloth, 21/-.

MOZART, WEBER AND WAGNER, with various other Essays on Musical Subjects. Crown 8vo, cloth, 21/-.

The above three books form a full and readable translation by Edwin Evans of the justly celebrated critical writings of Hector Berlioz issued under the title of "A Travers Chant."

BORODIN THE COMPOSER AND HIS MUSIC. A Descriptive and Critical Analysis of his Works and a Study of his Value as an Art Force. With many references to the Russian Kouchka Circle of Five—Balakirev, Moussorgsky, César Cui, Rimsky-Korsakov, and Borodin. By GERALD ABRAHAM. With music examples and 5 Portraits. Crown 8vo, cloth, 25/-.

LIFE OF JOHANNES BRAHMS. By FLORENCE MAY. Second Edition, Revised. Two Volumes, demy 8vo, cloth, 42/-.

This work still remains the most comprehensive single work on the composer published. It is based on material gathered at first hand during the course of several visits to the Continent, and its value as a personal document is enhanced by the author's own recollections and impressions of Brahms, which were the result of personal contact with and actual study under the great master.

VOCAL WORKS OF BRAHMS. In the Order of their Opus Number with Biographical, Analytical and other explanatory details, Review of Criticism, Special Translations and copious Information. By EDWIN EVANS. Demy 8vo, cloth, 42/-. (The companion volumes on the Piano, Organ and Chamber and Orchestral Works are out of print.)

LIFE OF CHERUBINI. By F. J. CROWEST. (Great Musicians Series.) Crown 8vo, cloth, 6/–.

CHOPIN'S GREATER WORKS (Preludes, Ballads, Nocturnes, Polonaises, Mazurkas). How they should be Understood. By J. KLECZYNSKI. Including Chopin's Notes for a "Method of Methods." Translated by N. JANOTHA. Second Edition. With music examples. Crown 8vo, cloth, 10/–.

HOW TO PLAY CHOPIN. The Works of Chopin, their Proper Interpretation. By J. KLECZYNSKI. Translated by A. WHITTINGHAM. Sixth Edition. Music Illustrations. Crown 8vo, cloth, 7/6.

Contains the cream of Chopin's instructions to his own pupils. To admirers of Chopin and players of his music we should say this book is indispensable.

FREDERIC CHOPIN, Critical and Appreciative Essay. By J. W. DAVISON. 8vo, 3/6.

CHOPIN THE COMPOSER AND HIS MUSIC. An Analytic Critique of Famous Traditions and Interpretations, as exhibited in the Playing of Great Pianists, Past and Present. By JOHN F. PORTE. With portrait. 193 pages, crown 8vo, cloth, 10/6.

HANDBOOK TO CHOPIN'S WORKS. A Detailed Account of all the Compositions of Chopin. Short Analyses for Piano Student and Critical Quotations from Writings of Well-known Musical Authors. Chronological List of Works, etc. By G. C. A. JONSON. Second Edition. Crown 8vo, cloth, 18/–.

"Here in one compact volume is all that is necessary to know about Chopin and his works except by the leisured enthusiast."

HANDEL'S MESSIAH. The Oratorio and its History. A Handbook of Hints and Aids to its Public Performance, with useful Notes on each Movement, as well as Numerous References and much Original Information. By J. ALLANSON BENSON. Boards, 6/6; paper, 4/–.

LISZT, COMPOSER, AND HIS PIANO WORKS. Descriptive Guide and Critical Analysis, written in a popular and concise style. By HERBERT WESTERBY, *Mus.Bac., Lon., etc.* 5 illustrations, 24 music examples. 336 pp., crown 8vo, cloth, 21/–.

ANALYSIS OF MENDELSSOHN'S ORGAN WORKS. A Study of their Structural Features. By JOSEPH W. G. HATHAWAY, *Mus.B. Oxon.* 127 Music Examples. Portrait and Facsimiles. Crown 8vo, cloth, 12/6.

HOW TO INTERPRET MENDELSSOHN'S "SONGS WITHOUT WORDS" (the celebrated "Lieder ohne Worte"). A Readable and Useful Guide for All. Gives the Piano Students helpful Insight into the first Principles of Form in Music. By CHARLES W. WILKINSON. With portrait and facsimile of MS. Crown 8vo, cloth, 6/-; paper, 3/6.

MOZART: a Commemorative Address read before the Positivist Society. By V. LUSHINGTON. 8vo, 3/-.
Mozart and Religion.

THE SONATA: Its Form and Meaning, as Exemplified in the Piano Sonatas by Mozart. A Descriptive Analysis, with Musical Examples. By F. HELENA MARKS. 8vo, cloth, 18/-.

QUESTIONS ON MOZART'S SONATAS. By F. HELENA MARKS. Aid and Companion to the Study of the Author's work, "The Sonata: Its Form and Meaning as Exemplified in the Piano Sonatas by Mozart." Paper covers, 2/6.

RACHMANINOFF. An Exhilarating Biographical Study of this Genius of the Keyboard. By WATSON LYLE. Preface by LEFF POUISHNOFF. Two Portraits and List of Works. Crown 8vo, cloth, 18/-.

FRANZ SCHUBERT, Man and Composer. A Vivid Story of a Charming Personality. By C. WHITAKER-WILSON. With Original Translations into English of eight Well-known Schubert Songs, together with the Music for the Voice. Portraits and Illustrations of Schubert and his Friends. Crown 8vo, cloth, 15/-.

HENRY SMART'S ORGAN COMPOSITIONS ANALYSED. By J. BROADHOUSE. Crown 8vo, cloth, 7/6.

WAGNER'S TEACHINGS BY ANALOGY. His Views on Absolute Music and of the Relations of Articulate and Tonal Speech, with Special Reference to "Opera and Drama." By EDWIN EVANS. Crown 8vo, cloth, 6/-; paper, 3/6.

WAGNER'S Ring des Nibelungen. The Story of Wagner's "Ring" for English Readers. By N. KILBURN, *Mus.Bac.*, *Cantab.* Crown 8vo, paper, 2/-.

HOW TO UNDERSTAND WAGNER'S "RING OF THE NIBELUNG." Being the Story and a Descriptive Analysis of the "Rheingold," the "Valkyr," "Siegfried" and the "Dusk of the Gods." With Musical Examples of the Leading Motives of Each Drama. By GUSTAVE KOBBE. Together with a Sketch of Wagner's Life. By N. KILBURN, *Mus.Bac. Cantab.* Seventh Edition. Crown 8vo, cloth, 12/6.

Description and analysis go hand in hand with the narration of the story. Musical examples are given as aids to the identification of the leading motives and an index makes it easy for any reader to turn up any particular motive instantly.

WIT AND MIRTH: OR PILLS TO PURGE MELANCHOLY. Edited by THOMAS D'URFEY. Introduction by CYRUS L. DAY. A facsimile reproduction of the 1876 reprint of the original edition of 1719-20. This is a famous collection of songs, poems and ballads, all with music, a few dating from the Elizabethan period, but the majority from the second half of the 17th century. Three Volumes, £8.

OUT-OF-PRINT BOOKS.

Positive Microfiches can be supplied of the following books where the printed editions are out of print They must be used in conjunction with a reader (usually found in large libraries).

HISTORY OF THE VIOLONCELLO, Viola da Gamba, etc., with Biographies of all the Most Eminent Players, 1915. By E. VAN DER STRAETEN, 50/-.

ORCHESTRAL

THE CONDUCTOR, THE THEORY OF HIS ART. By HECTOR
BERLIOZ. Translated by J. BROADHOUSE. With 41 Diagrams
and Examples. Crown 8vo, cloth, 8/6; paper covers, 5/–.

INSTRUMENTS AND ART OF THE ORCHESTRA. An Introductory Study. With Table showing Range of each Instrument. By P. W. DE COURCY-SMALE, *Mus.Bac.* 8vo, boards, 6/–.

METHOD OF INSTRUMENTATION. How to Write for the
Orchestra and Arrange an Orchestral or Band Score. Illus-
trated with Music Examples and various large folding Charts
and Index. By EDWIN EVANS. Demy 8vo, cloth, two volumes.
Vol. I. How to Write for Strings, Arrangement of Scoring and
Preparation of Parts. With Charts. 10/–.
Vol. II. How to Write for Wood, Brass and Drums, and
Arrange a Band Score. With large folding Charts. 10/–.

NOTES ON CONDUCTORS AND CONDUCTING. By T. R.
CROGER, *F.R.G.S.*, *F.Z.S.*, also the Organising and Conducting of Amateur Orchestras, with three full-page Illustrations of the various "Beats" and Plan of the Orchestra.
Revised and Enlarged. Crown 8vo, paper covers, 3/6.

ON CONDUCTING. By RICHARD WAGNER. Translated by E.
DANNREUTHER. Crown 8vo, boards, 12/6.

ORCHESTRAL AND BAND INSTRUMENTS. A Short Account
of the Instruments used in the Orchestra, and in Brass and
Military Bands. By G. F. BROADHEAD, *Mus.B. Dunelm*,
L.Mus.T.C.L. With 24 Illustrative Music Examples. Post
8vo, cloth, 5/–, paper covers, 3/–.

ORCHESTRAL WIND INSTRUMENTS, Ancient and Modern
Being an Account of the Origin and Evolution of Wind
Instruments from the Earliest Times. By U. DAUBENY, 11
plates illustrating 61 Instruments or Parts. 8vo, cloth, 25/–.

PRACTICAL GUIDE FOR THE CONDUCTOR and Useful
Notes for the Orchestra. By F. W. DE MASSI-HARDMAN. With
Music Examples and Diagrams. 3/–.

ORGAN

ART OF ORGAN ACCOMPANIMENT IN THE CHURCH SERVICES. What to Do and what to Avoid: being a Guide to the Organist in the effective rendering of the Music. By WALTER L. TWINNING, *F.R.C.O.* Boards, 3/6.

THE CHURCH ORGAN. An Introduction to the Study of Modern Organ Building. By NOEL A. BONAVIA-HUNT. With 40 diagrams. A reprint of the well-known book first published in 1920. Demy 8vo, cloth, 25/-.

THE EARLY ENGLISH ORGAN BUILDERS and their Works, from the Fifteenth Century to the Period of the Great Rebellion By DR. E. F. RIMBAULT. Post 8vo, boards, 12/-.

THE INFLUENCE OF THE ORGAN IN HISTORY. By DUDLEY BUCK. Crown 8vo, boards, 4/-; paper covers, 2/-.

INTERNATIONAL REPERTOIRE GUIDE (Historical, Educational and Descriptive) to Foreign, British and American Works. By HERBERT WESTERBY. 4to, cloth, 25/-.

Describes the best Organ Music of foreign countries as well as of Britain and America.

A large and beautifully presented quarto work, fully illustrated by thirty-six plates on fine art paper, comprising seven English and sixteen foreign organs, thirty-one portraits, and illustrations of the houses of Bach and Handel.

LECTURE ON THE PEDAL ORGAN. Its History, Design and Control. By THOMAS CASSON. With folding Diagram. 8vo boards, 8/6.

MODERN ORGAN BUILDING. By WALTER & THOMAS LEWIS (Organ Builders). Practical Explanation and Description of Organ Construction with especial regard to Pneumatic Action and Chapters on Tuning, Voicing, etc. Third Edition, Revised. 116 Illustrations, including 76 Drawn to Scale and Reproduced from actual Working Drawings. 4to, cloth, 42/-.

MODERN ORGAN TUNING, The How and Why, Clearly Explaining the Nature of the Organ Pipe and the System of Equal Temperament, together with an Historic Record of the Evolution of the Diatonic Scale from the Greek Tetrachord. By HERMANN SMITH. Crown 8vo, cloth, 15/-.

NEW ORGAN PRINCIPLES AND THEIR INTERPRETATION. A Guide to and Suggestions on Phrasing and Registration with a view to improved Organ Playing. By TERENCE WHITE. With 54 music examples. Demy 8vo, paper covers, 4/-.

THE ORGAN FIFTY YEARS HENCE. A Study of its Development in the Light of its Past History and Present Tendencies. By Francis Burgess, *F.S.A., Scot.*, 1908. Demy 8vo, 3/6.

ORGAN OF THE ANCIENTS FROM EASTERN SOURCES (Hebrew, Syriac and Arabic). By Henry George Farmer, *M.A., Ph.D., Carnegie Research Fellow.* Foreword by Canon F. W. Galpin. With numerous Illustrations. 8vo, cloth, 42/-.

REFORM IN ORGAN BUILDING. By Thomas Casson. Demy 8vo, 3/-.

SOME CONTINENTAL ORGANS and their Makers. With Specifications of many of the fine Examples in Germany and Switzerland. By James I. Wedgwood. Post 8vo, boards, 8/6.

TECHNICS OF ORGAN TEACHING. A Handbook which treats of Special Points in Organ Teaching Examinations, together with Test Questions. By R. A. Jevons. Boards, 3/6.

TECHNICS OF THE ORGAN. An Illuminative Treatise on many Points and Difficulties connected therewith. Special Treatment of Rhythm, Minimisation of the Use of Accessories, Extemporisation, Expressive Regulation of Organ Tone and Accompaniment. By Edwin Evans, *F.R.C.O.* With over 100 Music Examples. 4to, 15/-.

PIANO

THE APPROACH TO LISZT. A Course of Modern Tonal-Technique for the Piano, in the form of Graded Studies from the Moderately Difficult to the Master Stage. By HERBERT WESTERBY, *Mus.Bac. Lond., F.R.C.O., etc.* Folio, 5/6.

Preliminary Studies in Touch and Phrasing in all Keys. Based on the Scales and Broken Chords.

Intermediate Studies in Sequential, Wrist and Preparatory Arpeggio Work in the Black and White Key Positions.

Advanced Sequential Studies on the Black Keys, with Sixteen Excerpts from Liszt's Piano Works. The Master Works: Fifty-eight Excerpts from Liszt.

THE ART OF TUNING THE PIANOFORTE. A New Comprehensive Treatise to enable the Musician to Tune his Piano upon the System founded on the Theory of Equal Temperament. By HERMANN SMITH. New Edition, Revised. Crown 8vo, boards, 8/6.

THE ARTIST AT THE PIANO. Essays on the Art of Musical Interpretation. By GEORGE WOODHOUSE. 8vo, cloth, 6/–.

The celebrated pianist, Paderewski, after reading the manuscript of this stimulating volume, wrote: "The booklet is quite a remarkable work and a really valuable contribution to the philosophy of pianistic art."

THE BYRD ORGAN BOOK, for Piano or Organ. A Collection of 21 Pieces (Pavans, Galliards, etc.), by William Byrd, 1543–1623, edited from the Virginal MSS., and now first published in Modern Notation. By M. H. GLYN. 7/6.

DELIVERY IN THE ART OF PIANOFORTE PLAYING, On Rhythm, Measure, Phrasing, Tempo. By C. A. EHRENFECHTER. Crown 8vo, cloth, 6/–.

THE DEPPE FINGER EXERCISES for Rapidly Developing an Artistic Touch in Pianoforte Playing, Carefully Arranged, Classified and Explained by AMY FAY (Pupil of Tausig, Kullak, Liszt and Deppe). Folio, English or Continental Fingering, 2/–.

EXTEMPORISING AT THE PIANO MADE EASY. A Manual for Beginners in Musical Composition. Hints and Aids for the "From Brain to Keyboard" Composer. By REV. E. H. MELLING, *F.R.C.O.* 8vo, 2/–.

HOW TO ACCOMPANY AT THE PIANO. By EDWIN EVANS. (Plain Accompaniment, Figurated Accompaniment and Practical Harmony for Accompanists.) 172 Music Examples. Crown 8vo, cloth, 7/6.

HOW TO PLAY 110 FAVOURITE PIANO SOLOS. Being the 4 Series complete in 1 vol. of "Well-Known Piano Solos: How to Play them with Understanding, Expression and Effect." By CHARLES W. WILKINSON. Crown 8vo, cloth, 12/6.

HOW TO STUDY THE PIANOFORTE WORKS OF THE GREAT COMPOSERS. By HERBERT WESTERBY, *Mus.Bac.* Handel, Bach, Haydn, Scarlatti, Mozart, Clementi, C. P. E. Bach, Beethoven. With 123 Musical Examples. Crown 8vo, cloth, 12/6.

The following issued singly, paper covers:
HANDEL, 1/–; D. SCARLATTI, 1/–; J. S. BACH, 1/6; C. P. E. BACH AND HAYDN, 1/–; CLEMENTI, 1/–; MOZART, 1/6.

INDIVIDUALITY IN PIANO TOUCH. By ALGERNON H. LINDO and J. ALFRED JOHNSTONE. Crown 8vo, 2/6.

INTRODUCTION TO RUSSIAN PIANO MUSIC. By HERBERT WESTERBY, *Mus.Bac.Lond., F.R.C.O., L.Mus.T.C.L.*, 1/–.

NATURAL TECHNICS IN PIANO MASTERY. A Complete and authoritative Manual, covering every Phase of Piano Playing and Study—tracing in simple Steps for the Student's Guidance the aesthetic Steps as well as the technical Problems leading from Beginning Stages to Concert Artistry. By JACOB EISENBERG. 55 illustrations. Crown 8vo, cloth, 12/6.

PIANOFORTE TEACHER'S GUIDE. By L. PLAIDY. Translated by F. R. RITTER. Crown 8vo, boards, 3/–; paper, 2/–.

REEVES' VAMPING TUTOR. Art of Extemporaneous Accompaniment, or Playing by Ear on the Pianoforte, Rapidly Enabling anyone having an Ear for Music (with or without any Knowledge of Musical Notation) to Accompany with Equal Facility in any Key. Practical Examples. By FRANCIS TAYLOR. Folio, 2/–.

THE STUDENT'S GUIDE TO THE ART OF TEACHING THE PIANOFORTE. By CYRIL R. H. HORROCKS, *L.R.A.M., L.T.C.L., A.R.C.M.* With an Extensive and Carefully Graded List of Studies and Course of the Great Masters. Numerous Musical Examples. Second edition, Revised. Crown 8vo, cloth, 10/–.

A SYSTEM OF STUDY OF SCALES AND CHORDS. Being Chapters on the Elements of Pianoforte Technique. By B. VINE WESTBROOK, *F.R.C.O.* Numerous Examples. Revised edition. 8vo, 3/–.

B

**TECHNICAL STUDY IN THE ART OF PIANOFORTE PLAY-
ING** (Deppe's Principles). By C. A. EHRENFECHTER. With
numerous music examples. Fourth Edition. Crown 8vo,
cloth, 6/-.

CONTENTS: Position—Arm—Wrist—Fingers; Touch (Tone Pro-
duction); Legato; Equality of Tone; Tension and Contraction;
Five Finger Exercises; Skips; The Scale; Arpeggio Chords; Firm
Chords; High Raising of the Arm; Melody and its Accompani-
ment; Connection of Firm Chords; The Tremolo; The Shake
(Trill); The Pedal; Fingering.

TOUCH, PHRASING AND INTERPRETATION. By J. ALFRED
JOHNSTONE. Crown 8vo, cloth, 7/6.

TECHNICAL AND THEORETICAL

THE ART OF MODULATING. A Series of Papers on Modulating at the Pianoforte. By HENRY C. BANISTER. With 62 Music Examples. Crown 8vo, cloth, 6/–; paper covers, 3/6.

THE ART OF MODULATION. A Handbook showing at a Glance the Modulations from one Key to any other in the Octave, consisting of 1,008 Modulations. For the Use of Organists and Musical Directors. Edited by CARLI ZOELLER. 4to, paper covers, 5/–.

COMPEND OF MUSICAL KNOWLEDGE. By PERCY BAKER, *F.R.C.O., L.Mus.T.C.L.* Being a Guide with Notes, Hints and Articles on the Study of Examination Questions. Crown 8vo, cloth, 6/–; paper, 3/6.

ELEMENTARY MUSIC. A Book for Beginners. By DR. WEST-BROOK. With Questions and Vocal Exercises. Crown 8vo, cloth, 4/–; paper, 2/–.

ESSENTIALS IN MUSIC STUDY FOR EXAMINATIONS. A Helpful Guide both for the General Student and Candidates for Junior and Intermediate Examinations. By REV. E. H. MELLING, *F.R.C.O.* Cloth, 5/–; paper covers, 2/6.

EXAMINATION CANDIDATE'S GUIDE to Scale and Arpeggio Piano Playing (with Tests). All that is required for the Various Exams. By WILSON MANHIRE, *L.R.A.M.* 3/–.

EXAMINATION TEST QUESTIONS. Containing spaces for the Pupils' Written Answers. By WALTER L. TWINNING, *F.R.C.O.* No. 1, Musical Notation and Time; No. 2, Formation of Scales; No. 3, Ornaments; No. 4, Intervals, 9d. each.

EXERCISES IN FIGURED BASS AND MELODY HARMON-IZATION. By JAMES LYON, *Mus.Doc.* 4to, 3/6.

EXAMPLES OF FOUR-PART WRITING FROM FIGURED BASSES AND GIVEN MELODIES. By JAMES LYON, *Mus.Doc.* 4to, 5/6.

These exercises are printed in open score so as to be of use in score reading tests. This volume forms a key to "Exercises in Figured Bass" by the same author (see above).

EXERCISES ON GENERAL ELEMENTARY MUSIC. A Book for Beginners. By K. PAIGE. Part I, 1/6; Part II, 2/–.

GUIDE FOR THE YOUNG COMPOSER. Hints on the Art of Composition, with Examples of Easy Application. By REV. E. H. MELLING, *F.R.C.O.* 2/6

HANDBOOK OF MUSICAL FORM. For Instrumental Players and Vocalists. By E. VAN DER STRAETEN. With Musical Examples, 205 pages. Crown 8vo, boards, 8/6; paper, 4/-.

THE HARMONISING OF MELODIES. A Textbook for Students and Beginners. By H. C. BANISTER. Third Edition, with numerous Music Examples. Crown 8vo, limp cloth, 5/-.

HARMONY, EASILY AND PROGRESSIVELY ARRANGED. Presenting in a Simple Manner the Elementary Ideas as well as the Introduction to the Study of Harmony. With about 300 Music Examples and Exercises. By PAUL COLBERG. Crown 8vo, cloth 7/6; paper covers, 3/6.

HOW TO COMPOSE WITHIN THE LYRIC FORM. By EDWIN EVANS, *F.R.C.O.* Described for the General Reader, Practically Exemplified for the Musician and Reduced to Precept for the Student. With 60 Music Examples. Crown 8vo, cloth, 6/-.

HOW TO HARMONIZE MELODIES. With Hints on Writing for Strings and Pianoforte Accompaniments. By J. HENRY BRIDGER, *Mus.Bac.* With Music Examples. Crown 8vo, cloth, 6/-.

HOW TO MEMORISE MUSIC. By C. F. KENYON. With numerous Music Examples. Crown 8vo, cloth, 6/-.

HOW TO PLAY FROM SCORE. Treatise on Accompaniment from Score on the Organ or Piano. By F. FETIS. Translated by A. WHITTINGHAM. With forty pages of Examples. Crown 8vo, cloth, 7/6.

This popular and useful book might have been entitled "The Art of Making Arrangements for the Organ or Pianoforte from Full Orchestral and Other Scores." It contains all that is necessary to know upon this subject.

THE MODAL ACCOMPANIMENT OF PLAIN CHANT. A Practical Treatise. By EDWIN EVANS, Senior, *F.R.C.O.* Part I, Theoretical; Part II, Practical School of Plain Chant Accompaniment, consisting of 240 Exercises, with an Appendix of Notes. Crown 8vo, cloth, 12/-.

MODERN CHORDS EXPLAINED. (The Tonal Scale in Harmony.) By ARTHUR G. POTTER. Music Examples from Debussy, Strauss and Bantock. 8vo, cloth, 4/-; paper covers, 2/-.

MUSICAL ACOUSTICS. (Student's Helmholtz), or the Phenomena of Sound as Connected with Music. By JOHN BROADHOUSE. With more than 100 Illustrations. Fifth Impression. Crown 8vo, cloth, 21/–.

MUSICAL ANALYSIS. A Handbook for Students. By H. C. BANISTER. With Music Examples. Crown 8vo, limp cloth, 5/–; paper covers, 2/6.

MUSICAL EXPRESSIONS, PHRASES AND SENTENCES, with their Corresponding Equivalents in French, German and Italian. By F. BERGER. 8vo, cloth, 5/6.

MUSICAL PRONOUNCING DICTIONARY. By DR. DUDLEY BUCK. Eighth Edition, with the Concise Explanation and Pronunciation of each Term. Edited and Revised by A. WHITTINGHAM. Crown 8vo, 1/6.

PRIMARY COURSE IN THE RUDIMENTS OF MUSIC, With Hints on Answering Questions (Written Work) for All Examinations in the Primary, Elementary and Preparatory Grades. By WILSON MANHIRE, *L.R.A.M.*, etc. 2/–.

THE RUDIMENTS OF GREGORIAN MUSIC. By FRANCIS BURGESS, *F.S.A.*, *Scot.* Crown 8vo, limp cloth, 2/6; paper, 1/6.

RUDIMENTS OF MUSIC, Set forth in Graded QUESTIONS with ANSWERS, for Use of Candidates preparing for the Examinations of R.A.M., R.C.M. and T.C.L. By B. HOWARTH, *L.R.A.M.* and *A.R.C.M.* Crown 8vo, 2/–.

The Answers are always on the right hand page and can be covered over if desired, the Questions being on the corresponding left hand pages.

SCHUMANN'S RULES AND MAXIMS FOR YOUNG MUSICIANS. Sewed, 6d.

STEPS IN HARMONY. With Copious Explanatory Examples and Graded Test Exercises. A Handbook for Students. By DR. CHURCHILL SIBLEY. With Music Examples throughout. Crown 8vo, boards, 6/–.

THE STUDENT'S BOOK OF CHORDS. With an Explanation of their Inversions and Resolutions. By PASCAL NEEDHAM. Crown 8vo, 1/6.

STUDIES IN HISTORICAL FACTS AND MUSICAL FORM.
Being a Guide and Note Book for a more Systematic Preparation of the General Knowledge Papers now set at the Universities and Colleges of Music. By PERCY BAKER. Crown 8vo, 3/–.

STUDIES IN MODULATION for Practical and Theoretical Purposes. By PERCY BAKER, *F.R.C.O.*, etc. 3/–.

102 TEST QUESTIONS ON THE GENERAL RUDIMENTS OF MUSIC. In Groups of Six each Lesson, for Written or Oral Use. By WILSON MANHIRE, *L.R.A.M.* 6d.

THEORY OF MUSIC FOR YOUNG MUSICIANS. With Answers given to all the Questions, and a Dictionary of necessary Musical Terms. By MARY SHARP. 1/6.

TRANSPOSITION AT SIGHT. For Students of the Organ and Pianoforte. By H. E. NICHOL. Fourth Edition, with numerous Musical Exercises. Crown 8vo, 2/–.

The practice of transposing upon the lines here laid down develops the "mental ear," quickens the musical perception and gives ease in sight reading; as it is evident that, if the student can *transpose* at sight, he will not have much difficulty in merely *playing* at sight. Free use is made of the tonic sol-fa as well as the standard notation in many musical examples.

VIOLIN AND
STRINGED INSTRUMENTS

ADVICE TO VIOLIN STUDENTS. Containing Information of the Utmost Value to every Violinist. By WALLACE RITCHIE. Crown 8vo, cloth, 7/6; paper, 5/-.

AIDS TO ELEMENTARY VIOLIN PLAYING. By JEFFREY PULVER. Crown 8vo, cloth, 12/6.

ART OF HOLDING THE VIOLIN AND BOW AS EXEMPLIFIED BY OLE BULL. His Pose and Method proved to be based on true Anatomical Principles. By A. B. CROSBY, *M.D., Professor of Anatomy*. Portrait, Diagrams and Illustrations. 8vo, cloth, 6/-.

ART OF VIOLONCELLO PLAYING. Tutor in Three Books. By E. VAN DER STRAETEN. Text in English and French. 4to. Book I, 3/6; Book II, 4/-; Book III, unpublished.

BIOGRAPHICAL DICTIONARY OF FIDDLERS. Including Performers on the Violoncello and Double Bass. By A. MASON CLARKE. 9 Portraits. Post 8vo, cloth, 25/-.

BOW INSTRUMENTS, their Form and Construction. Practical and Detailed Investigation and Experiments regarding Vibration, Sound Results, and Construction. By J. W. GILTAY. Numerous Diagrams. 8vo, cloth, 16/-.

CHATS WITH VIOLINISTS. By WALLACE RITCHIE. Crown 8vo, cloth, 10/6.

GERMAN VIOLIN MAKERS. By FRIDOLIN HAMMA. A Critical Dictionary of German Violin Makers with a Series of Plates Illustrating Characteristic and Fine Examples of their Work. Translated by Walter Stewart. 64 pages of text and 80 plates in half-tone, 12 × 10 inches, cloth, 105/-.

This book is written by one of the most prominent experts in Europe, this status assuring the importance of his contribution to violin connoisseurship.

About 80 fine German instruments are represented in the plates of this book, the majority by two views, whilst many are extra-illustrated by separate scroll pictures. Good, representative examples of the German masters were selected for the purpose of providing the most informative illustrations, and a short descriptive general treatment accompanies each maker's name in the text. The arrangement of the text is on an alphabetical plan.

Fridolin Hamma's book is one of the most important contributions of our time to violin literature, a work which no connoisseur or maker should miss.

THE HISTORY OF THE VIOLIN and other Instruments Played on with the Bow from the Remotest Times to the Present. Also an Account of the Principal Makers. Coloured Frontispiece and numerous Illustrations and Figures. By W. SANDYS, *F.S.A.*, and S. A. FORSTER. Demy 8vo, cloth, 35/-.

This well-known book, first published in 1864, is especially valuable in connection with the instrument makers of the English school, and is the chief literary source of information concerning our old native craftsmen. It is good to bear in mind that as Simon Forster was a skilled and experienced instrument worker, the technical notes to be discovered in the pages of this book in which he collaborated are worthy of attention.

HOW TO BECOME A PROFESSIONAL VIOLINIST. By OSCAR CREMER. Preface by CHARLES WOODHOUSE. Crown 8vo, cloth, 8/6.

HOW TO MAKE A VIOLIN. By J. BROADHOUSE. Revised Edition. Folding Plates and many Diagrams, Figures, etc. Crown 8vo, cloth, 12/6.

CONTENTS: Introduction—The Parts of the Violin—On the Selection of Wood—The Tools required—The Models—The Mould—The Side-pieces and Side Linings—The Back—Of the Belly—The Thickness of the Back and Belly—The Bass Bar—The Purfling—The Neck—The Finger-board—The Nut and String Guard—Varnishing and Polishing—Varnishes and Colouring Matter—The Varnish—A Mathematical Method of Constructing the Outline—The Remaining Accessories of the Violin.

HOW TO PLAY THE FIDDLE. For Beginners on the Violin. By H. W. and G. GRESSWELL. Eighth Edition. Crown 8vo, 2 parts, paper covers, 1/6 each.

HOW TO REPAIR VIOLINS and other Musical Instruments. By ALFRED F. COMMON. With Diagrams. Crown 8vo, cloth, 8/6.

AN IMPORTANT LESSON TO PERFORMERS ON THE VIOLIN. By the Celebrated TARTINI. Portrait. Translated by DR. BURNEY, issued originally in 1779, together with the original Italian. 8vo, boards, 7/6.

INFORMATION FOR PLAYERS, Owners, Dealers and Makers of Bow Instruments, also for String Manufacturers. Taken from Personal Experiences, Studies and Observations. By WILLIAM HEPWORTH. Crown 8vo, cloth, 8/6.

A MUSICAL ZOO. Twenty-four Illustrations displaying the Ornamental Application of Animal Forms to Musical Instruments (Violins, Viol da Gambas, Guitars, Pochette, Serpent, etc.). Drawn from the Carved Examples by HENRY SAINT-GEORGE. Cloth, 6/-; paper, 3/6.

NOTABLE VIOLIN SOLOS: How to Play Them. Three Series (consisting of 44 descriptive Articles in all). By E. VAN DER STRAETEN. 2/6 each series. Also complete in boards, with Portraits, 15/-.

NOTICE OF ANTHONY STRADIVARI. With a Theoretical Analysis of the Bow and Remarks on Tourte. By F. J. FETIS. Demy 8vo, cloth, 21/-.

First published in 1864, this book is of particular value because the facts and ideas contained in it were given to the author by the great violin maker Vuillaume.

OLD VIOLINS AND VIOLIN LORE, Famous Makers of Cremona and Brescia, and of England, France and Germany (with Biographical Dictionary), Famous Players, and Chapters on Varnish, Strings and Bows, with 13 full-page plates. By H. R. HAWEIS. Demy 8vo, cloth, 25/-.

A delightful informal account of famous makers, players and collectors. In matters pertaining to old violins, the author is known as a specialist and, moreover, one who writes in a pleasant flowing style, which cannot be said of all specialists. He discourses about Italian, French and English violins, about varnish, strings, bows, violin dealers, collectors and amateurs. There are some fine plates, a dictionary of violin makers and a bibliography. This book is one for reading, and also for reference, and in its lighter pages for recreation.

PLAYING AT SIGHT FOR VIOLINISTS and Others in an Orchestra. Valuable Hints and Aids for its Mastery. By SYDNEY TWINN. Post 8vo, 3/6.

70 PREPARATORY VIOLIN EXERCISES for Beginners in the First Position, carefully Graduated, Supplementary to the First Instruction Book. By WILSON MANHIRE, *L.R.A.M., A.R.C.M., etc.* 2/6.

ROYSTON'S PROGRESSIVE VIOLIN TUTOR (with Illustrations giving Correct Position for Hand, Wrist and Fingers). Folio, 3/-.

SKETCHES OF GREAT PIANISTS AND GREAT VIOLINISTS. Biographical and Anecdotal, with Account of the Violin and Early Violinists. Viotti, Spohr, Paganini, De Beriot, Ole Bull, Clementi, Moscheles, Schumann (Robert and Clara), Chopin, Thalberg, Gottschalk, Liszt. By G. T. FERRIS. Third Edition. Crown 8vo, cloth, 12/6.

TONAL SCALES AND ARPEGGIOS FOR VIOLIN. Introductory to the Unusual Intonation and Finger-grouping of Advanced Modern Music. By SYDNEY TWINN. Folio, 3/-.

TREATISE ON THE STRUCTURE AND PRESERVATION OF THE VIOLIN and all other Bow Instruments. By Jacob Augustus Otto. Together with an Account of the most Celebrated Makers and of the Genuine Characteristics of their Instruments. Translated by John Bishop. Fourth Edition. Crown 8vo, cloth, 12/6.

VIOLIN AND CELLO BUILDING AND REPAIRING. By Robert Alton. With 82 diagrams and 2 plates. Crown 8vo, cloth, 16/-.

Robert Alton gave forty years to the study of the violin and its construction and was in close touch with makers, both amateur and professional, all over the world. He invented several tools by reason of actual experience at the bench, and has proved that they are entirely satisfactory for the work required of them. He has carried out innumerable repairs to violins, bows and cellos, and is entirely practical.

THE VIOLIN AND OLD VIOLIN MAKERS. Being a Historical and Biographical Account of the Violin. By A. Mason Clarke. With Facsimile of Labels used by Old Masters. Crown 8vo, cloth, 10/-.

VIOLIN HARMONICS. What They Are and How to Play Them. By C. E. Jacomb. Crown 8vo, cloth, 6/-.

THE VIOLIN HUNTER. The Life Story of Luigi Tarisio, the Great Collector of Violins. By W. A. Silverman. Demy 8vo, cloth, 30/-.

Luigi Tarisio had a fascinating career in the early 19th century discovering Cremona violins in Italy where they had lain forgotten and gathering dust for years, and bringing them to the dealers and collectors of Paris and London. In this book on violin romance and history, the author tells Luigi Tarisio's life story for the first time.

VIOLIN MANUFACTURE IN ITALY and its German Origin. By Dr. E. Schebek. Translated by W. E. Lawson. Second Edition. Square 12 mo, cloth, 6/-

VIOLIN TECHNICS, or How to Become a Violinist. Exact Instructions, Step by Step, for its Accomplishment with or without a Teacher. By "First Violin." 3/6.

VIOLINIST'S ENCYCLOPÆDIC DICTIONARY. Containing the Explanation of about 4,000 Words, Phrases, Signs, References, etc., Foreign, as well as English, used in the Study of the Violin, and also by String Players generally, by F. B. Emery, *M.A.* New and enlarged edition. 246 pp., crown 8vo. Cloth, 15/-

WELL-KNOWN VIOLONCELLO SOLOS. How to Play Them. Three Series. By E. van der Straeten. 2/6 each series. Also complete in cloth, with Portraits, 18/-.

VOCAL

THE AMATEUR VOCALIST. A Guide to Singing. With Useful Hints on Voice Production, Song Preparation, etc. By WALTER L. TWINNING, *F.R.C.O.* Post 8vo, limp cloth, 2/-.

THE ART OF VOCAL EXPRESSION. A Popular Handbook for Speakers, Singers, Teachers and Elocutionists. By the REV. CHAS. GIB. Crown 8vo, cloth, 5/-; paper, 2/6.

THE CENTRAL POINT IN BEAUTIFUL VOICE PRODUCTION. By H. TRAVERS ADAMS, *M.A.* 2/6.

ELEMENTARY LESSONS ON SIGHT SINGING. Combining the Staff and Tonic Sol-fa Notations. With Music Examples throughout. By J. W. ROSSINGTON, *L.R.A.M.* Cloth, 3/6; paper, 2/-.

HOW TO ATTAIN THE SINGING VOICE, or Singing Shorn of its Mysteries. A Popular Handbook for those desirous of winning Success as Singers. By A. RICHARDS BROAD. Crown 8vo, boards, 6/-.

HOW TO SING AN ENGLISH BALLAD. By E. PHILP. Eighth Edition. Crown 8vo, paper, 1/-.

HOW TO TEACH CLASS SINGING, and a Course of Outline Lessons which illustrate the psychological principles upon which successful tuition is based. By GRANVILLE HUMPHREYS, Professor of the Art of Teaching, Voice Production, etc., at the T.S.-F.C.; late Lecturer in Class Singing at the Training School for Music Teachers. Numerous Music Illustrations. Cloth, 10/-.

OBSERVATIONS ON THE FLORID SONG. Or Sentiments on the Ancient and Modern Singers. By P. F. TOSI. Translated by Mr. Galliard. With music examples. A reprint of this celebrated book, first published in 1743. Crown 8vo, 25/-.

SIMPLICITY AND NATURALNESS IN VOICE PRODUCTION. A Plea and an Argument. By EDWIN WAREHAM. Crown 8vo, cloth, 2/6.

SPEECH DISTINCT AND PLEASING, or Why not Learn to Speak Correctly? A clear description of the mental and physical qualities on which the art of good speaking is founded. By FRANK PHILIP. 162 pages, Crown 8vo, cloth, 7/-; paper covers, 4/-.

SUCCESS IN AMATEUR OPERA. Instructions on Auditions, Equipment of the Society and the Conductor, Allocation of Rôles, Rehearsals, Training of Soloists, Diction, Conducting, etc. By HUBERT BROWN. Including a Section on Stage Management, by H. G. TOY. Crown 8vo, cloth, 6/-.

TEXTBOOK OF VOCAL TRAINING AND PREPARATION FOR SONG INTERPRETATION. With a Section showing how to Determine Accurately by Pitch and Curve Graphs the special Suitability of Songs selected for particular Vocal Requirements. Music Illustrations and Descriptive Diagrams. By FRANK PHILIP. 8vo, cloth, 15/-.

THE THROAT IN ITS RELATION TO SINGING. By WHITFIELD WARD, *A.M.*, *M.D.* Illustrations. Crown 8vo, cloth, 5/-.

TREATISE ON THE TRAINING OF BOYS' VOICES. With Examples and Exercises and Chapters on Choir-Organization. Compiled for the Use of Choirmasters. By GEORGE T. FLEMING. Crown 8vo, cloth, 5/-; paper, 2/6.

TWELVE LESSONS ON BREATHING AND BREATH CONTROL for Singers, Speakers and Teachers. By GEORGE E. THORP. Crown 8vo, paper covers, 3/-.

TWENTY LESSONS ON THE DEVELOPMENT OF THE VOICE. For Singers, Speakers and Teachers. By G. E. THORP. Crown 8vo, limp cloth, 2/6.

THE VOICE AND SINGING. Practically Explained, Condensed but Comprehensive Treatise, designed principally for Students and Amateurs, by an Experienced Singer and Teacher (C. W. PALMER). Cloth, 5/-; paper, 2/6.

VOCAL SCIENCE AND ART. Hints on Production of Musical Tone. By REV. CHAS. GIB. The Boy's Voice, Muscular Relaxation, Art of Deep Breathing, Elocution for Ordination Candidates. Crown 8vo, cloth, 6/-.

VOCAL SUCCESS, or Thinking and Feeling in Speech and Song, including a Chapter on Ideal Breathing for Health. By the REV. CHAS. GIB. Crown 8vo, cloth, 5/-; paper covers, 2/6.

VOICE PRODUCTION FOR ELOCUTION˙AND SINGING. By REV. E. H. MELLING. Music Examples. 31 pages, f'cap 8vo, cloth, 4/-; paper covers, 2/-.

Printed in Great Britain by
Lowe and Brydone (Printers) Limited, London, N.W.10

66 a